GHOST STORIES

of

NEW JERSEY

D1562248

A.S. Mott

LONE
PINE

Lone Pine Publishing International

The Publisher: Lone Pine Publishing International
Distributed by Lone Pine Publishing
1808 B Street NW, Suite 140
Auburn, WA 98001
USA

Websites: www.lonepinepublishing.com
www.ghostbooks.net

National Library of Canada Cataloguing in Publication Data

Mott, A. S. (Allan S.), 1975-
Ghost stories of New Jersey / A.S. Mott.

ISBN-13: 978-976-8200-16-7
ISBN-10: 976-8200-16-2

1. Ghosts--New Jersey. 2. Tales--New Jersey. I. Title.

GR110.N5M68 2006   398.209749'05   C2006-903204-1

Photo Credits: Every effort has been made to accurately credit photographers.
Any errors or omissions should be directed to the publisher for changes in
future editions. The photographs and illustrations in this book are repro-
duced with the kind permission of the following sources: Iwona Adamus
(p. 36); Bernardsville Library (p. 190); Galina Dreyzina (p. 27); James
Goldsworthy (p. 32); Jarrett Green (p. 49); Bonita Hein (p. 202); Library of
Congress (p. 66: HABS NJ,3-MOUHO,8-3; p. 71: HABS NJ,3-MOUHO,8-6;
p. 156: USZ62-94848; p. 188: USZ62-59619); Jim Parkin (p. 81); Richard
Perks (p. 137); Jose Carlos Pires (p. 215); Wally Stemberger (p. 12); Ryan
Stowinsky, www.stuofdoom.com (p. 110, p. 127); Charissa Wilson (p. 22).

The stories, folklore and legends in this book are based on the author's
collection of sources including individuals whose experiences have led them
to believe they have encountered phenomena of some kind or another. They
are meant to entertain, and neither the publisher nor the author claims
these stories represent fact.

PC: P5

To Dave Gwilliam

Each day is a Gift

Contents

Acknowledgments 5

Introduction 6

The Little Devils
Part I: Mrs. Shrouds' 13th Baby 8

The Death of Hannah Caldwell 22

The Phantom Collie 29

The Express Train to Hell 34

A Bad First Date 39

Burlington 64

The Little Devils
Part II: Rachel Letton's British Soldier 74

The Hookerman 94

Buckeye 106

The Dutchman 132

The Gentleman Thief 140

The Devil's Tower 160

The Strange Fate of Antoine Le Blanc 178

The Tavern Owner's Daughter 188

The Little Devils
Part III: The Devils Revealed 215

Acknowledgments

Many thanks to Volker Bodegom, Sheila Quinlan and Carol Woo for their work on editing this manuscript. I would also like to thank Trina Koscielnuk for her fine work in putting this book together.

Introduction

Having had the opportunity to visit schools and read from my books to kids of all ages, I've come to appreciate how fine an art storytelling is. There are few things as difficult and rewarding as keeping an audience of people—young or old—enthralled as you tell them an exciting tale or two. It's a tradition that goes back farther than any form of written literature and it's how most of the stories in this book originally came to be. Long before anyone thought to write them down, people told many of these stories over campfires, during moments of quiet boredom and any other time a good scary story seemed appropriate.

Ghost stories—no matter where you are from—are a vital part of a place's oral tradition, whether based on historical fact or on an urban legend about the spooky old house at the end of the street. In the cases of stories like these, the story itself is often less important than the manner in which it is told. The very nature of oral storytelling asks that you adapt your tale to whoever it is you are telling it to, a fact that inevitably results in many different versions of the same story.

There are essentially two types of books about ghosts—those that do their best to ignore the oral tradition and find out the "truth" behind these legends and those that recognize that, when it comes to ghost stories, the truth is at best a very subjective thing and the real fun to be had is in the telling of the tales. I've always fallen in the latter camp—to quote the famous line from John

Ford's classic western *The Man Who Shot Liberty Valance,*
"When the legend becomes fact, print the legend."

This is less a book for people who want to have their
personal beliefs about the supernatural supported in print
than it is a collection of entertaining stories based on
supernatural folklore found throughout the state of New
Jersey. Some of the stories are quite old, dating back to the
Revolutionary War and even earlier, while others take
place just a few decades ago. Some are long, some are
short, but they all share the common thread of having
first been established in stories people shared among
themselves long before they ever made it to print in books
like this one.

In the end my greatest hope is that you come away
from the book having been entertained. It would be nice if
you felt you had learned a thing or two as well, but ulti-
mately this is a book meant to hit your heart and your gut,
rather than your head. And if there happens to be a story
or two in here that sticks inside your head, then tell it to
someone else—not only is it really fun, but it ensures that
the oral tradition continues to live on.

The Little Devils
Part I:
Mrs. Shrouds' 13th Baby

Donny and Max were sitting in the middle of their makeshift clubhouse, reading comic books and occasionally engaging in their long, ongoing debate of whether or not Batgirl was cuter than Supergirl. Donny felt she was, but Max disagreed.

"This is stupid," sighed Donny. "We've been having this same argument for a month now. We're not going to change our minds, so it's obvious what we should do."

"Agree to disagree and talk about something else?" suggested Max.

"No," snorted Donny. "We'll ask Andy when he gets here, and he'll decide."

"So when is he coming?" asked Max.

"He said he was going to be here after his piano lesson," answered Donny.

"Did he find those books he was telling us about?"

"Yeah. He's going to be bringing them with him."

It was around noon on a warm Saturday afternoon in July of 1972. Donny and Max had just turned 13 that summer, and their friend Andy was just three weeks away from becoming a teenager himself. They had known each other for as long as they could remember, having grown up together on the same block in the small town of Estelville. Back when they were all 10 they had scavenged the town for free building supplies and had built their clubhouse in the middle of a wooded area not far from their homes. There, Donny and Max spent most of their time debating every trivial matter that occurred to them, leaving Andy to inevitably decide which one of them was right.

"If I were Superman," Donny decided as he flipped through the latest issue of *Adventure Comics*, "I think I would dump Lois and start dating Wonder Woman."

The boys' comic book discussions used to focus strictly on which heroes were stronger than the others and who would prevail in theoretical battles to the death. Now, without them having noticed the change, they spent most of the time talking about the heroes' girlfriends or female counterparts.

Max thought about Donny's declaration and concluded that it was sound. "Yeah," he agreed. "Lois is pretty, but she's useless in a fight. Wonder Woman is just as beautiful and she can also back Superman up when he's fighting against Lex Luthor. I bet that would be real handy for him."

At that point an intricate knock was heard coming from their clubhouse door. Donny got up from his seat and opened the door, letting Andy inside.

Andy was carrying a heavy bag over his shoulder. It appeared to be filled with several leather-bound books. Before he could set it down, Donny was already asking him the major question of the day.

"Who's cuter, Batgirl or Supergirl?"

Andy scrunched up his face as he pondered this dilemma. "Are we including their secret identities or just how they look in their costumes?"

"As a whole," answered Max.

"Then I'd have to say Batgirl," said Andy.

"Told ya!" Donny yelled at Max as he celebrated his moral victory.

"You're both crazy," argued Max.

"Ah, you just like Supergirl because she reminds you of Tina DeMarco," Donny teased. Tina was a classmate of theirs who Max had had an unacknowledged crush on since the fourth grade.

Andy smiled at this remark and finally dumped the heavy bag of books onto the clubhouse's rickety wooden floor.

"Wow," said Donny, "how many did you find?"

"Six," answered Andy. "I don't know if all of them will be helpful, but I figured I'd bring them over anyway."

"Okay," said Max, "put them on the table and we'll get this meeting in order."

Andy set the books on the small wooden table they had rescued from someone's curb. The three of them then grabbed the stools they had taken from their respective homes and sat around the table. Donny grabbed the door-knob he used as a gavel and banged it against the table to bring the meeting to order.

"We now begin the fourth meeting of the Estelville Monster Society," said Donny. "Our recorder, Max Walston, will now read the minutes from our last meeting."

Max cleared his throat and began reading from the notebook in front of him. "Our last meeting was held this previous Tuesday at 4:30 PM. We began by reading the minutes from our last meeting followed by Donny asking Andy to settle our argument over which member of Josie & the Pussycats looked better in her Pussycat outfit, Josie or Melody. Andy decided that Donny's choice of Josie was the clear winner." Max looked up from his notebook. "What is it with you two and redheads?"

The clubhouse was in the middle of a wooded area not far from their homes.

"Never mind that," said Donny. "Just read the rest of the minutes."

"After that the rest of the meeting was spent discussing our plan to become world-famous adventurers by becoming the first society to ever successfully capture the Jersey Devil. It was decided that to capture the Devil we would have to know everything we could about the creature, so Andy volunteered to go to his grandfather's house and find every book he could that mentioned it. We also decided that at the following meeting we would look over these books and gather the necessary information. The meeting then ended so we could all go home and eat."

"Thank you, Max," said Donny. "Now I think we should get to the main business of today's meeting as outlined during our last meeting. I see Andy Carter, our chief researcher, has found six books for us to go through. I propose that we all start reading them right now and then tell each other what we have found out. All those in favor?"

"Yea," Andy and Max agreed in unison.

"All those opposed? No one? Then it's unanimous. Let us begin reading and report what we have discovered within the next hour." He banged the doorknob on the table to make this decision official, and each of them grabbed one of the books and started reading.

Despite their love for comic books, none of the boys were what you would call voracious readers. All three of them struggled to make it through the hour without falling asleep or putting down their book in favor of the latest issue of *The Brave and the Bold*. They were all relieved when Max announced that the hour was finally up and they could begin talking about what they had all just learned about New Jersey's most famous mythical monster.

"Who wants to start?" asked Donny. Both of his friends stayed quiet and cast their eyes down toward the table, so he sighed and said, "All right, I guess I'll go first." He reopened his book and turned to the pages he had been studying. "According to this, this is the true legend of the Jersey Devil…"

*   *   *

If anyone had ever decided to go around the town of Leeds Point, New Jersey, and ask the people who lived there to describe their neighbor, Mildred Shrouds, chances are the same word would have been used over and over again. That word would not have been *smart*, because most everyone agreed that she was a very simple woman. Nor would it have been *kind*, because she was not known to ever be patient or charitable with others. *Pretty* wouldn't have sprung to anyone's lips, but then neither would have *ugly*, as she was a woman with the kind of neutral features that inspired little in the way of adoration or revulsion—hers was a face that so lacked distinction, it faded from memory the second she turned away from you. No, the one word that would have sprung to everyone's mind would have been *fertile*. For there was no doubt that Mildred Shrouds was the most fertile woman in the entire town.

She and her husband, Mister (who had been given that name by his proud father so that "Everyone, no matter their status, will always call my son Mister."), had had 12 children within a span of eight years (a number made possible by the birth of twin girls, Madame and Mademoiselle), which had left her with only a scant handful of months during that time in which she was not in some stage of pregnancy. To say she was, by that point, sick of the whole process was an understatement, to say the least. When the very familiar signs pointed to her being once again with child—her 13th—hers was not an expression of joy, but instead a loud curse of frustration and horror.

"I cannot bear it," she moaned to her friend Dora. "The thought of another nine months in this condition. I just delivered Monsieur a month and a half ago!"

"I would think you'd be used to it by now," said Dora. "You've been pregnant for as along as I've known you. I honestly can't think of you any other way."

"And that's the problem! I've grown so tired of living like this! I would love to someday be able to see my toes! Or to someday not be sickened by random smells I usually enjoy! And you would think that giving birth would be no problem after having done it so many times, but each one is as painful and agonizing as the last! And all of the children! I hate children! With their snotty noses and constant crying! 'Mommy, I need this—Mommy I need that!' It never ends with those little monsters!"

"If you hate them so much, then why have you had so many?" asked Dora.

"Because Mister loves them so much. Too many could never be enough for him. You should have seen him when Mister, Jr., was born! I thought such joy could never be topped, but with the birth of each child his happiness only increased. I had hoped that at some point his enthusiasm would sour—I figured it would happen when he ran out of names to give them, but then he started using the French variations, and I suspect he'll turn to Spanish or Italian when this child is born."

"Have you tried talking to him?"

"Of course! You don't think I haven't ordered him out of my bed following each and every child? But I love him so much, and he has those big brown eyes, and I always let him come back and a month later I'm having another one of his children. No," she decided, "the only way this is ever going to stop is if this 13th child is a monster—a real devil—the kind of nasty imp that makes all children look bad. It has to be a baby so evil that it will make my Mister never want to touch me ever again, on the chance it would be followed by something even more foul."

Dora laughed. "Be careful what you wish for, Mildred," she warned her friend. "Someone might be listening and make sure that it comes true."

Mildred sighed. "Dora, I'm counting on it."

As the months passed, Mildred eventually forgot about her conversation with Dora and no longer wished for her 13th child to be born such a holy terror that it would drive her husband from ever wanting another child ever again. She wished instead for apples, as many as Mister could supply. They were not a wealthy family, and fresh fruit was a luxury they could ill afford—especially with 14 mouths to feed—but Mister did everything he could to satisfy his wife's cravings.

Unfortunately, "everything he could" included venturing into a nearby orchard and pilfering a bushel to take home. Plagued by similar thieves over the years, the orchard's owner had decided to defend his crops by buying two very large guard dogs who didn't take kindly to people trespassing on their master's property.

"Nice doggies…" were Mister's last words.

Mildred couldn't fathom the position in which she had been left: a widow with 12 children and one more on the way in just a couple of months. She was able to keep the house because it had been left to the two of them by her parents when they died, but she had no savings and no idea how she was going to fend for herself or her many children.

She sent the three oldest children—Mister, Jr., and Miss who were eight and Sir who was seven—out to work any small job a person was willing to hand over to a child. The rest of her kids were too young for these jobs and, as a result, served no use for her, so she sent them to a local orphanage. That same fate awaited baby number 13, but it was a destiny the child seemed unwilling to meet, as it stayed inside her belly for a full month longer than it should have.

"Blast this foul child!" she cursed one morning when she was talking to Dora. "I swear it knows not to come out, because I'm going to get rid of it when it does."

"Don't you miss your babies, Mildred?" asked Dora, who had been against sending them away to the orphanage.

"I have never had so much peace in my life," answered Mildred. "With little Mister, Miss and Sir gone all day,

I have the house all to myself. It's wonderful! I couldn't be happier!"

"But don't you think your husband would disapprove?"

"He should have thought about that before he was savaged to death by those two beasts. I'm not responsible for being put into this position, but that doesn't mean I shouldn't take advantage of it and do something for myself."

"But everyone is saying such horrible things about you."

"Let them! I never noticed them being too terribly helpful when I was trying to take care of a dozen little animals," she retorted.

The next day Mildred finally went into labor. Too poor to pay for a doctor to attend to the birth, she had Dora take care of it instead. Despite all of her previous experience, she had been unprepared for the pain and misery that came during this particular delivery. The labor itself lasted 29 agonizing hours, each more miserable than the last. It felt as though the baby was not merely content to come out, but to do so in the slowest—most sadistic— manner possible.

Dora had not been prepared for what she saw when the baby's head finally appeared.

Mildred, even through her misery, still managed to notice the shocked look of horror on her friend's face. "What's the matter?" she asked in voice that alternated between a coarse whisper and agonized scream.

"Um…" Dora hesitated. She didn't quite have the words required to answer such a question.

"You're scaring me," Mildred insisted. "What is—" she screamed as she pushed the baby the rest of the way out.

Dora cut the cord and wrapped the baby in the blanket. "Uh, Mildred," she finally spoke.

"What?" asked her exhausted friend.

"You remember when you said that you wished this child would be a 'real devil' so Mister wouldn't want to have any more children?"

"Vaguely. Why?"

"I think…I think you got your wish."

She handed the child to Mildred and she looked down at the baby and screamed. If the baby was human, then it was doing a masterful job disguising itself as something else. Where its nose and mouth should have been, there was instead a long canine snout—already filled with sharp little teeth. Its ears were long like a bat's, and its entire body was covered with a mat of brown fur. Its feet were cloven like a goat's, and its back was covered by a hard leathery substance that looked almost like a shell. Most shocking of all was the long tail that grew out of the base of the baby's spine.

Mildred fainted dead away, leaving a stunned Dora to figure out what to do with this "baby" all by herself. Until she could think of something else to do, she stuck it in a cupboard. This decision was a mistake; the crying sound that arose from the monster child was enough to rattle the shingles off of the roof. It was even enough to wake up Mildred, who, with Dora, discovered that the only way to calm the baby down was to hold it.

"What am I going to do?" asked Mildred. "The orphanage is never going to accept a beast like this, and there's no way I can raise it myself."

"I don't know what to tell you, Mildred," answered Dora.

Eventually Dora had to leave, and Mildred hid the new baby from her three remaining children when they returned from their jobs. As the children slept that night, she decided that her only option was to abandon the baby in the woods and hope that nature would sort everything out.

Holding the sleeping infant in her arms, she walked to the nearby woods and gently placed the baby on a nearby tree stump. She got about three steps away before the baby woke up and started crying in its distinctly monstrous way. Not knowing what else to do, she started running, praying that no one would see her returning home.

No one did, but that proved to be of little comfort when she awoke the next morning and discovered that somehow the baby had managed to return and now lay happily at the end of her bed. She tried abandoning it four more times, in increasingly hard-to-return-from locations, but the monster child found its way back each time. It appeared there was no way for her to get rid of it.

Not long afterward, the baby discovered what its teeth were for and took to biting Mildred's fingers whenever the opportunity presented itself. Those little teeth were sharp enough to draw blood and hurt like the dickens each time the baby nipped at her. Soon the biting and the deformed child's constant need for attention drove poor Mildred to consider infanticide. She fought those thoughts of murder for as long as she could, but eventually the little devil baby left her with no other option.

While her other children were at work, she went outside and found the axe Mister, Jr., used to chop wood for the stove. She took it into the house and hid it behind her back, then quietly approached the baby as it slept in its crib. As quietly as she could, she raised the axe over her head, but before she could bring it down, the baby awoke and surprised Mildred one last time.

The leathery shell on its back burst open and revealed itself to be a set of two bat-like wings. With them the baby flew out of the crib, past its mother and escaped out of the house by flying straight up the chimney.

The shock was too much for Mildred to bear, and she collapsed to the floor. Her three remaining children found her there. Dimly aware of their presence, she told them what she had just seen before succumbing to the injuries the shock had done to her heart...

To Be Continued

The Death
of Hannah
Caldwell

The British were coming, and James knew it. He had very little time left before they would be descending upon his farmhouse, just a few miles out of Elizabethtown. He spent that time trying to convince his wife to leave with him.

"No," she refused. "I will not leave the children alone here to the whims of that Hessian brute."

James had already sent their six oldest children away to a friend who had the resources to protect them, but his three youngest were incapable of making the journey and remained at the farm with their nurse and Abigail, a young orphan they had taken in following the death of her father at British hands.

"They'll be safe here," he insisted. "Yes, they mean to murder me, but even they would not be heartless enough to kill a group of defenseless children."

"That is a chance I am not willing to take."

"But Hannah—"

"James! You do not have time to argue with me. My mind is set and you do not have the time to change it." She turned and looked out the window of their living room. "Look, you can see the gleaming of their bayonets in the distance. They'll be here in less than half an hour. You must ride away to Morristown now, before it's too late."

James knew she was right. If he stayed, the British would catch him and execute him on the spot. He prayed that they would not be so barbaric as to seek vengeance against him by instead murdering his wife.

"I love you," he told her with a brief kiss before he turned and ran out of the house. He mounted his horse and spurred the animal into the fastest gallop it could manage. He did not turn his head to look back.

*   *   *

They called him the Rebel Priest.

James Caldwell had only been the pastor at Elizabethtown's Presbyterian Church for a few years when the Revolutionary War started. It took him no time at all to choose his side. His Scottish blood predisposed him to abhor any form of British tyranny. He joined the rebel army, where his services as an orator dedicated to rousing his fellow soldiers to action brought him to the attention of the leaders of both sides. To his fellow revolutionaries he was a great asset; his sermons served as exactly the kind of inspiration they needed when times got tough. For that same reason the British considered him a major irritant and put a price upon his head.

Thus, he found himself in the odd position of delivering sermons on the gospel of peace with two loaded pistols within reach of his pulpit. The bounty on his head also forced him to leave his home in Elizabethtown and find temporary shelter in nearby Springfield. He donated his parsonage to the army, which used it and his former church as a hospital for wounded soldiers. In late January 1780, the British burned both buildings to the ground.

Not content to remain hiding in Springfield, he moved to a farmhouse just outside of Elizabethtown. He stayed there until the British forces, led by a Hessian general named Knyphausen, took control of the town in June of that year and quickly made finding him their first priority.

Their march in pursuit of him was filled with acts of cruel terrorism as they burned down several houses they came across, but not before robbing their inhabitants of everything they had worth carrying.

But these acts of barbarism did not help the British cause, as word of them spread quickly and James discovered they were heading his way. He had no choice but to flee, but he would soon regret his inability to convince his wife to join him.

*   *   *

Hannah got ready for her impending uninvited visitors. First she took her family's most valuable possessions and hid them in a bucket at the bottom of their well, and then she went to her room and got dressed in the same clothes she would have worn to greet an honored guest.

"What are you doing, Mrs. Caldwell?" asked the children's nurse, who was confused by this strange gesture.

"I shall receive them like a lady, Doris," Hannah answered. "I shall not stoop to their level. If they are to come into my home, I shall welcome them as I would anyone one else."

"But they are barbarians," said Doris. "They'll have no appreciation for such a gesture."

"They won't harm a mother," Hannah insisted. "Even they won't sink that low."

Now fully dressed, she retrieved her baby and started nursing the tiny child. As her daughter suckled her breast, she sat facing her window and watched the British army, led by Knyphausen, march toward her home. "They shall respect a mother," she told herself.

Doris and Abigail entered her room and looked out the window. Hannah handed her baby daughter over to Doris as Abigail reported on the movements of the men outside.

"I see a man in red," she told them. "He's coming near the window. He has a—" But before the girl could say another word she was interrupted by a tiny explosion, followed by the sound of breaking glass. Abigail screamed as shards of the glass cut into her face, but her cries were drowned out by the shouts of Doris, who was still holding the Caldwells' baby daughter in her arms.

"Mrs. Caldwell!" she cried out. "Mrs. Caldwell!" With her blood on her hands, Abigail turned and saw Mrs. Caldwell lying still on her bed. The blood from the large red wound in the middle of her chest was already soaking through her dress and into the quilt underneath her.

She was dead.

At that moment a group of soldiers burst into the room through the door and the shattered window. Doris screamed at them, but they shoved her quickly out the door. Abigail stayed quiet and said nothing as they descended upon the body of the murdered woman and used their knives to cut away at her fine dress, searching for whatever trinkets of value she might have been keeping on her person. They found nothing, so they lifted up her body and carried it over to the house across the road. They then removed Doris and all of the children from the Caldwell home, set it ablaze and watched it until it had burned down to nothing but ash.

*   *   *

The British were coming, and James knew it.

James had seen the smoke from the fire in the distance, but he had mistakenly assumed that it was not coming from his house. Only later did he learn the horrible truth. Some men, on hearing such news, would become crippled by their grief, but he was not one of them; if anything, the callous murder of his wife only served as fuel that drove him in his fight against the British.

But her husband was not the only man inspired by Hannah Caldwell's death. Her murder became a symbol of the terrors of British tyranny and inspired many who were once reluctant to fight to join the cause at last.

Hannah was buried in the cemetery of the First Presbyterian Church, right next door to the Union County Courthouse. When James died a year later, shot by an American who many believed had been bribed to assassinate him, his body was buried right beside hers.

Many people who worked at the courthouse over the following centuries insisted that they had seen Hannah's ghost walking along the path that connects the building to the graveyard she resides in. Always described as looking serene and happy, her spirit leaves no indication of any kind of unhappiness or distress. She seems to have accepted her fate.

If she has ever communicated with anyone, then such a meeting has gone unrecorded. She has played no tricks on anyone or indulged in any of the antics other ghosts enjoy enacting when they want to get the attention of the living. She seems content to occasionally appear on the grounds and look around briefly.

Some people wonder if maybe there is pain behind her spirit's brief wanderings. They note that while her ghost is commonly seen, her husband's is not. In fact, James Caldwell has not been seen since his murder all those years ago. Perhaps he has been able to move on, but she has not, and that serenity noted in her ghostly face is really loneliness. No one knows for sure.

The
Phantom
Collie

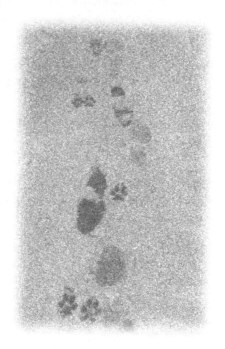

Unless you're a dog fancier with a specific interest in collies, chances are you're unfamiliar with the name Albert Payson Terhune. That wouldn't have been the case during the 1920s and '30s, when—thanks to a series of books he wrote about his pet collies—Terhune became a world-famous advocate for the breed. The first and most influential of these books, *Lad, A Dog*, was published in 1919 and has been in print nearly constantly since then. It detailed the adventures of a heroic Rough collie named Lad, who performed his daring deeds a good 19 years before Lassie made the scene in 1938 (courtesy of a short story by Eric Knight). Unluckily for Lad, Lassie quickly made it off the printed page into the world of film and television and eclipsed him in renown (though he would eventually be immortalized on celluloid in 1962 when a film version of *Lad, A Dog* hit theaters, 43 years after the book was first published).

A prolific writer who penned titles about a wide variety of topics, Terhune is best known for his collie books, largely because his passion for the breed allowed him to invest in those works a sense of pride and admiration that is palpable on every page. The line of dogs he raised on Sunnybanks, his New Jersey estate, still exists today as one of the premier examples of the breed, and he is largely regarded as the man responsible for crafting the collie's noble image and enduring popularity.

But what many of his admirers don't know is that three years before he published his most famous work, Terhune had an experience with one of his dogs that was unlike anything he ever wrote in his fiction. And though he never saw it himself, several of his friends and visitors to Sunnybanks reported having had several encounters with an animal that was not of this world.

It all started one March day in 1916. Terhune was at work at his typewriter when he heard the sound of a ferocious battle erupt from outside his window. He got up and looked outside and was horrified to see his two favorite dogs, Lad and Rex, tearing into each other with a savagery never previously suggested by their normal, everyday demeanors. Not knowing what else to do, Terhune ran to his closet and pulled out a large hunting knife and ran outside.

There he could see that Rex was clearly the aggressor and that Lad was merely attempting to defend himself. Terhune stood helpless for a second as he watched Rex lunge at Lad's throat. Rex had never acted with such ferocity—it almost seemed as if the creature was possessed by something unholy.

Knowing that he had to act fast to save Lad's life, Terhune ran to Rex and plunged the large knife into his side. Rex howled in pain and tried to turn and bite his master, but the wound was severe. The life ebbed out of him quickly.

Terhune was devastated over the loss of a favorite dog, especially considering how the behavior he had just witnessed defied any explanation. Rex and Lad had been raised together and had appeared to be the best of friends. Terhune had no idea what could have caused the one animal to turn so viciously on the other.

Lad was severely injured, but he was eventually nursed back to health and eventually inspired Terhune to write the first of his most famous books. But two

Rex remained faithful to his master for over 26 years.

years before that happened—a year after the attack took place—a friend of the writer arrived at Sunnybanks for a visit. He was surprised to see a dog who looked just like Rex sitting outside the house. What especially shocked him was that a large scar was clearly visible on the dog's side, right where Terhune had been forced to stab Rex.

When the friend told Terhune about what he had seen, he noted that the dog looked especially sad sitting where he was, his head and eyes bowed down in that way dogs affect when they know they've done something wrong. It seemed as though Rex was back and full of regret for his unexplained attack on Lad.

Not long after this first sighting, another friend of Terhune's was shocked when he approached the author's house and found him sleeping in a chair on the front porch. It was not the sight of Terhune taking a nap that surprised him, but rather the fact that the phantom collie was sitting at his feet.

Once again, the ghostly animal looked abashed as it stared pleadingly up at his sleeping master, his eyes full of an obvious desire for some kind of forgiveness. The sight of him caused Terhune's friend to shout out to Rex's master, who awoke with a start, but it was too late. Rex's spirit had vanished, apparently cursed to remain forever unseen by the one person he needed to revisit the most.

Several more visitors to the estate spotted Sunnybanks' phantom collie over the years, but Terhune himself never saw the ghostly creature. Sightings of Rex's spirit lasted all the way until 1942, which—not coincidentally—was the year that his master died. With Terhune gone there was no chance for Rex to earn his forgiveness, which would explain why his spirit never returned to Sunnybanks again.

Or maybe this sad story has a happy ending after all. Perhaps when Terhune died, his spirit was finally able to see the guilty pet who had spent the past 26 years trying to get his attention. Perhaps Terhune was able at last to bestow upon Rex the forgiveness he had been waiting for all along.

The Express
Train to Hell

It was going to be a cold night, which was why Duncan was sipping liberally from the small flask of whiskey he kept on him at all times. Usually Newark's Central Station was a lot busier—even at this late an hour—but tonight it was as quiet as it was cold. Although he knew other railroad employees had to be around, they were nowhere to be seen, and for the first time since he started working at the station seven years ago he felt like he was there all by himself.

A veteran of the Civil War, Duncan was a fellow who looked far older than his actual age. Most people, when they saw him, assumed he was a man in his late 50s, when the truth was that he had just turned 35. His premature aging could at least in part be blamed on the flask from which he was currently sipping, a fondness for heavily fried foods and an extreme sense of nervousness that he had picked up while fighting against the Confederates. It made little sense for a man who jumped at any loud noise to work at a train station, because it meant having the life scared out of him on nearly an hourly basis, but he was not the type of man who could afford to be choosy about how he made his living.

For once the station was nearly silent—an almost unheard of occurrence, even with the hour approaching midnight. With a long, arm-stretching yawn, he walked down the train platform to the small ticket kiosk where he spent most of his time. He stepped inside the small booth, sat down and looked over to the calendar hanging to his right. In five minutes it was going to be May 10, 1872—a day, he could tell, that was going to be as tedious as any other.

His slumber ended with the sound of an approaching train.

He looked down at the schedule in front of him and saw that no trains were going to be arriving for another two hours. With any luck, he could hope to catch a quick nap before someone bothered him with a ticket request. That moment seemed like the perfect opportunity to lie back in his chair and find out. He closed his eyes, yawned once again and started to drift off into dreamland.

His slumber ended with the sound of an approaching train. He marvelled at how deeply he had slept for time to have passed so quickly, but he was confused when he checked his pocket watch and saw that it was just turning midnight, only five minutes had passed.

"There's no train coming in at midnight," he said to himself as he rechecked the schedule and made sure he was right. He was. And though it wasn't uncommon for a train to come in ahead of schedule, it was invariably by just a few minutes—not two hours. "I better see what's going on," he muttered as he walked out of the ticket booth.

The sound of the oncoming train was much louder outside of the kiosk. He realized that the train must still be far off in the distance, because he couldn't see it on the tracks. But as he stood there and waited, the sound grew louder and louder while the train remained out of sight.

Within a minute it sounded as though the train was passing right beside the platform, but Duncan could not see it. As he heard the phantom train whistle past him, he stuck a hesitant hand off into the air above the tracks. He felt the sensation of wind passing through his fingers, but nothing even remotely resembling a train.

Duncan felt his body tingle with a sensation he did not like. His arm began to hurt, and his nerves were busy telling him that something was about to happen to his heart.

Two hours later, the scheduled train rode into the station. The passengers who disembarked in Newark discovered the dead body of an apparently middle-aged man. In one hand he held a flask, while the other was clasped to his chest.

*   *   *

On the 10th day of every month throughout the 1870s, Central Station in Newark, New Jersey, was visited by a phantom express train whose origin was completely shrouded in mystery. By the decade's end, hundreds of people had seen and heard the ghost train pass through the station, but no one had ever been able to figure out why it appeared or where it had come from. There were rumors, of course. One told of a railway conspiracy to keep the news of a devastating train crash a secret; another suggested that the train was one that had been destroyed by the Confederates during the Civil War. Neither of these theories was ever backed up by any serious evidence.

Eventually there came the day when the phantom locomotive did not pass by the station, and it has not been seen or heard since. To this day no one has been able to solve the mystery of its strange, if short-lived, existence.

A Bad
First Date

Dinner had not gone well.

When Jeremy and Diane had arrived at the restaurant, the hostess refused to seat them immediately because they didn't have a reservation, which enraged Jeremy because he had made a reservation just that afternoon. After he had shouted at the poor woman for a full five obscenity-filled minutes, he produced his cell phone to prove to her that he had called them.

"There!" he said triumphantly, showing her that the number he had called was still stored in his phone's memory.

"That's not our phone number," she said with a frown.

"Yes it is," he insisted.

"Sir," she replied through gritted teeth, "I have worked here for five years—I know our phone number when I see it."

"Look," he said angrily, "I called this number and spoke to someone who took my reservation."

"And where did you get that number?" she asked him.

"From the phone book," he answered. "Where else?"

The woman bent down behind her station and produced the local phone book. She opened it up to the page where the restaurant was listed and studied it. When she found what she was looking for she put her finger on it and showed it to Jeremy. "Is that the number you called?" she asked coldly.

"Yes!" he answered. " I told you!"

"Sir," she said with the kind of smile reserved for those situations when a person is able to put a jackass in his proper place, "that's the number for the restaurant listed below this one. You made a reservation at a Denny's.

I'm sure if you leave right now you'll be able to make it over there before your table is filled."

During all of this fuss, Diane had been standing in front of the restaurant's fish tank, pretending that she had nothing to do with the crazy, red-faced, shouting man all of the other diners were trying not to stare at. It took everything she had in her not to laugh when the hostess managed to cut him off at his knees.

Jeremy was so embarrassed that he didn't even try to apologize. Instead he just turned away from the smiling woman, walked over to Diane and asked her if they could leave.

"Sure," she said. "No problem."

The two of them had just met 45 minutes earlier when he had arrived at her door to pick her up for the evening. The date had been set up by a friend of Diane's who worked with Jeremy and who had insisted that the two of them were made for each other. Neither of them was too fond of the idea of going on a blind date, but they also both had issues about dying alone, unmarried and unloved, so they agreed that it wouldn't hurt to meet just once for dinner and a movie.

Both of them had been holding their breath when Diane had opened her front door, and both of them had exhaled with relief when they saw that they both met each other's standards for physical attractiveness. Diane was small and fit, with long blond hair and a clear and (artificially) tanned complexion; Jeremy was tall and thin, with a thick head of brown hair that was obviously real and not a toupee (Diane having long ago learned how to spot even the most convincing of hair pieces).

Leaving the restaurant, Diane stayed quiet while Jeremy fumed with the rage that can only come from someone proving to the rest of the world that you're an idiot. They got into his aging sports car and drove in silence to the Denny's where he had made a reservation. It was a good thing he did, because the place was packed.

"We don't normally reserve tables," the hostess at the door informed him when he told her who he was, "but since you were the first person to actually call in and ask for one, I couldn't say no. I saved you the best booth in the house. It's far enough away from the kitchen that you can barely smell the grease." She then led them to a dark, secluded booth in the far corner of the restaurant, where they sat down and silently perused their menus.

"I bet the food here is better anyway," Jeremy said as he studied the list of entrees.

"Yeah, and I bet the other restaurant wasn't considerate enough to include pictures of all their dishes in their menu for its customers who can't read," she said with a tiny smirk.

"They have a steak sandwich," he said, "and that's good enough for me."

He saw her wince. "What's the matter?" he asked.

"Nothing," she replied, shaking her head.

"No, I saw that look on you face. What's wrong?"

She hesitated before continuing. "I'm just not too comfortable with the meat thing."

"You're a vegetarian?" he asked, pronouncing the word in a way that made it sound like a combination of *communist* and *heretic* in five syllables.

"Vegan, actually," she admitted.

"What's the difference?"

"Vegetarians still eat eggs and drink milk," she explained. "Vegans don't eat anything animal related."

"You don't drink milk?" he asked her incredulously.

"Nope."

"And you don't eat eggs?"

She shook her head.

"But everything on this menu comes with eggs," he told her, "including the desserts."

She laughed at this last comment, which made him smile.

When their waitress arrived at their table, he ordered the steak sandwich with eggs over easy and she ordered the house salad without dressing.

"No dressing?" he asked after the waitress had left them alone again.

"A girl has to watch her figure. Dressing is nothing but added fat."

"But without it, all you're getting is lettuce," he said as he grimaced.

"I like lettuce," she said firmly.

"I guess you'd have to, not eating meat and all. And you know what? You're the first vegetarian—sorry—*vegan* I've gone out with."

"That can't be true," she said disbelievingly. "There are a lot of us out there."

"Not in the circles I run in. Most of the people I know assume that anything leafy on their plate is there just to decorate the meat."

This remark made her laugh again, and Jeremy hoped he had managed to make her forget what had happened in the other restaurant less than half an hour ago.

The waitress came back with their drinks, which they sipped at slowly during the uncomfortable silence that followed. "So, Diane…" Jeremy searched his brain for something to say. "Marnie told me that you have a very interesting job."

"Some would say so," she said with a smile. "But I bet she wouldn't tell you what it was."

"That's right. She said I'd have to find out for myself."

"She probably thought you wouldn't believe it unless I told you myself."

"So are you going to keep me in suspense or what? I know you don't run one of those web sites where you sell nude pictures of yourself—I checked. Beyond that, I don't have a clue."

"I'm an animal psychic," she told him in a way that made it clear that she wasn't joking.

Unfortunately for Jeremy, he was taking a drink from his beer at that very moment, and he gasped and choked on it when he heard the words, *animal psychic.*

"Are you all right?" she asked as his face turned a dark shade of red.

He struggled to get the words out. "I'm…fine…"

It took him a full two minutes to stop coughing and return to a somewhat normal state. During that time everyone in the restaurant had turned to look in their direction, mildly curious to see who was dying in the dark corner booth.

"I wish I could say you were the first guy to do that after I told him what I do for a living," she said, "but I don't think you would even make the list of the first 10."

"Just to make sure that the lack of oxygen didn't affect my memory," he said in a hoarse voice, "you did say that you were an animal psychic, right?"

"That's right."

"And when you say 'animal psychic,' you mean that you are a psychic who works with animals?"

"Yes."

"But that's crazy!" He blurted out the words before he could think better of not saying it.

If she was offended, she didn't show it. He realized that she had probably gotten this response quite a lot over the years.

"It's why I'm a vegan. It's hard to eat an animal once you've read its mind and discovered how much it wants to live."

Jeremy struggled to think of something to say in response. "How does a person end up doing this kind of work?" he asked. It was the only thing he could come up with.

"Well, it's a gift isn't it? You don't choose it—it chooses you. Personally, I always thought I'd make a kickass receptionist, but the powers that be gave me the ability to read animals' minds, so I feel sort of obligated to do their bidding."

"And how much does an animal psychic make these days?" he asked, genuinely curious.

"I cleared just over $85,000 after taxes last year," she answered.

Alerted again by the sound of someone choking, the other diners once more turned to see what was happening in the far corner booth.

"Smaller bites," shouted out one helpful soul.

"And chew each one 25 times," added another.

"Did you say '$85,000'?" he asked after having once again regained his composure.

"Yeah, but that was a fairly slow year. Usually I make more."

"Don't tell me," he said, holding his hand up. "I don't think I can handle any more choking."

"I take it this is the first time you've ever dated someone who makes more money than you," Diane said with a smile.

"How would you know that?" he asked.

"Easy," she said. "I know how much Marnie makes, and since she's your boss it doesn't take much brain power to figure out that—even in our sexist society—she'd be earning more than you do. Does it make you uncomfortable to go out with someone who out-earns you?"

Jeremy lied. "Of course not. This is the 20th century," he answered.

"Twenty-first," she corrected him.

"Right," he said. "I keep forgetting we're in a new one."

Those words hovered in the air as the waitress arrived with their food. Jeremy dug into his poorly cooked steak while Diane demurely grazed on her salad. They both seemed a bit grateful for the distraction. Both tried to eat as slowly as they could, but eventually they were both staring at empty plates and faced another attempt at conversation.

"Have you ever been to the Cineplex in Atco?" he asked her.

"Why? Is that where we're going after this?"

"Yeah. My brother-in-law, Barry, owns the place, so I've got free passes to see movies there all year."

"How far a drive is that from here?"

"About 30 minutes going down the Burnt Mill Road."

"Isn't that a long way to drive for a free movie? We're only a few minutes from another theater right here."

"I also get free popcorn," he told her. "Plus there's something along the way I can show you. I think you'll find it really interesting."

"What's that?"

"You'll just have to wait and see." He smiled as he started pulling out his wallet to pay the check.

Diane pulled a credit card from her purse and beat him to the punch. "I've got this."

"But—" he protested.

"I insist. You should save your money. I know you don't have a lot to spend on fancy meals."

"But this is *Denny's*," Jeremy argued.

"Don't worry about it. I'll let you pay next time, if we decide to see each other again. That is if McDonald's isn't fully booked for the next six months," she teased.

*   *   *

A part of Jeremy wanted to just take Diane home right away and spare the both of them another two and a half hours spent together, but he was worried about what she would say to Marnie the next time they talked. He didn't want his boss to think he had treated her friend rudely, so he turned onto the Burnt Mill Road and prayed that the rest of the date would go much more smoothly.

"So what's this 'interesting thing' you wanted to show me? Can you at least give me a hint?" she asked.

He turned down the radio, which he had set to a hard rock station, and tried to hide his smile, remembering how many times this particular stunt of his had been successful in the past.

"Do you know the legend about this road we're on?"

"No. Did some gang members shoot some people who flashed them their high beams?"

He shook his head. "No, this road is haunted."

This revelation didn't quite get the response Jeremy was expecting.

"Oh please," she sighed. "I don't believe in that junk."

"What are you talking about?" he asked, slightly dumbfounded.

"Ghosts and all that stuff. It's all nonsense."

"But you're an *animal psychic,*" he said disbelievingly.

"So? What has that got to do with it?"

Jeremy was so taken aback by this question that it took him a minute to respond to it. "It just seems... strange...that you would believe that you have the ability to read animals' minds, but you don't believe in ghosts."

"Why should that be strange? The two things have nothing to do with each other. Psychic abilities are a scientifically proven fact, while ghosts are just supernatural nonsense. Anybody can tell you that."

"Do you know the legend about this road we're on?"

Jeremy stayed quiet and kept his eyes on the road while he tried to decide whether or not to turn around and take her home right then and there.

Diane noticed she had offended him and instantly felt guilty. "But I like hearing a good story," she said sweetly, "even if it isn't true."

"No," he said petulantly. "There's no point now. You've ruined the mood."

"Oh, come on. Please?"

"No."

"Don't be like that," she said. "I promise I'll be a very receptive audience."

Jeremy looked over at her and decided he might as well give it a go, even though he knew it wouldn't have the effect on her he had come to expect over the years. So he turned off the radio and starting talking in the voice people adopt when they want to be perceived as spooky and mysterious. "It all happened a long time ago, before either of us was born—"

She interrupted him. "That's convenient. That way we'd have to study old newspapers or something to find out if it was true or not."

"Look," Jeremy said, reverting back to his normal speaking voice, "if you don't want me to tell this story I won't tell it. It's not like I care."

"I'm sorry, please go on. It's very good so far."

He growled under his breath. "Fine, like I was saying, this all happened a long time ago, before either of us was born, which may seem convenient, but—heck—the same can be said about almost everything you'll read about in any history book—"

"Good point," she admitted.

"They say it was a warm summer night like this one—"

Diane couldn't help herself. "Okay, who's 'they'?" she asked. "And it's nearly winter outside. I saw you shivering while we were walking from the restaurant to the car."

Jeremy's knuckles whitened as his hands tightened their grip on his steering wheel. "They," he answered, "are the people who tell the story—"

"So, in other words, you?"

"Among others, yes," he said through gritted teeth. "And I know that it's cold outside, but I'm used to telling the story in the summer, when it's not."

"Okay," she shrugged. "It's no big deal."

Neither of them spoke for a full minute.

"I thought you were telling that story?" she asked when the tension became a bit too heavy to bear.

Jeremy looked over at her and almost said something rude, but he thought better of it and decided to make one last attempt to tell her his surefire, guaranteed-to-thrill ghost story. "I forgot where I was," he admitted before he started.

"They were saying it was a warm summer night like this one, only it wasn't because it's almost winter out," she reminded him.

"Thanks," he said testily. "It was a warm summer night and there was a boy who lived with his parents in a house along this road. His name was Timmy, and he was deaf in one ear—"

"Which—"

"The right one," he answered before she had time to ask her question. "You said you weren't going to interrupt."

"The sign of a good story is a wealth of detail," Diane said. "Anyone can tell you that."

"I'll keep that in mind." He sighed before he went on. "He was eight years old and he was a mischievous little kid who seldom listened to his parents—"

"That's not fair, he probably couldn't hear them half of the time."

"What?"

"You said he was deaf in his right ear. I bet the only reason he didn't do everything they said was that he only heard half of what they told him."

"Why half?"

"It just makes sense, doesn't it? If you can only hear out of one ear, it stands to reason that you'll only hear half of what everyone else does."

"I don't think it works like that."

"Are you a doctor?"

"No."

"Then I guess we'll just have to agree to disagree. Now go on, you were unfairly labeling the poor hearing-disabled boy as a troublemaker."

"I wasn't labeling him as anything—I was just saying that he sometimes acted up by doing things he knew he shouldn't."

"Like what?"

"Like sneaking out of bed at night and going outside to play while his parents were asleep."

"Okay, that is pretty bad."

"See? I told you. Anyway, one night he snuck out of the house and started playing with his big red ball in the family's driveway. He was dribbling it around when it hit a rock and bounced into the middle of the road. At that same time a group of kids were driving in a stolen car, drinking and smoking dope. They were all too stoned to immediately notice the little boy run out in front of them, and he didn't hear the car coming toward him because he was deaf in that one ear. Those delinquents screamed something fierce when they felt the car hit something and saw a small body fly up into the air in front of them. They didn't bother to stop to find out what they had done, and they only found out when they were arrested a few hours later. Timmy's parents heard the accident happen from inside their bedroom, and they rushed out and found their son dead in the middle of the street."

"That's horrible. I don't think I could ever recover from something like that if it happened to me."

"Yeah, they moved," Jeremy said quickly, wanting to get to the good part of the story. "So, ever since then, this road has been haunted by Timmy's spirit, and they say that the best way to see him is to get his attention by honking your horn really loud and blinking your high beams on and off three times in a row. Do you want to try and see if we can get his attention?"

"Go ahead." Diane shrugged dismissively.

Jeremy wondered if he should even bother. Usually when he told this story the girls he was with were so into it that they almost expected to see something after he honked his horn and flashed his lights, so they always jumped a foot or two into the air when he then turned and shouted "Boo!" at them as loudly as he could. But Diane was clearly unimpressed by the story and obviously wasn't going to fall for such a juvenile trick. He decided instead that he would pretend as though he was doing it as a lark and remain completely cool and nonchalant when Timmy failed to appear in front of them, as though he were a scientist who had just observed the negative result of his latest experiment.

Still driving down the road he pressed down hard on his horn and flashed on his high beams.

"That's once," he said aloud. "That's twice," he continued, unaware that Diane had stopped paying attention to him and was busy reapplying her lipstick. "And this makes three," he said with the final flash of his lights.

"AHHHHHHHH!!!!!!!!!!!"

He hadn't intended to scream like that, but he also hadn't intended to see a small boy jump in front of his car at that moment. He slammed on his brakes as quickly as he could, and his car skidded on the frosty road.

"What the hell's the matter with you?" Diane shouted at him when the car finally stopped.

Jeremy turned and saw a jagged red line smeared across her face. "Oh my god, are you bleeding?" he asked, raising his hand to her face.

She pushed his hand away. "No, you idiot. It's just lipstick. Now answer my question before I lose it."

"I think I hit a kid!" he answered her. With a growing sense of panic, Jeremy jumped out of his car and searched the road for the body of his unfortunate victim. Diane climbed out of the car and looked with him. After a couple of minutes both of them concluded that there was no one to be found.

"I swear I saw a kid jump in front of the car," Jeremy insisted. "I thought I killed him for sure."

"Wow," she said admiringly, "you're really good. You almost had me convinced there for a minute. You should become an actor."

"What are you talking about?"

She rolled her eyes with a laugh. "Oh, come on, you don't actually expect me to believe you really saw that ghost you were talking about."

"It was a ghost?" asked Jeremy, the possibility only now occurring to him.

"No, it was you thinking you could get me to scream like some dumb girly-girl. I got something to tell you, fella, I have five older brothers; there isn't anything you can do that will scare me."

"It was a ghost," Jeremy said to himself, completely oblivious to what Diane was saying. "The story is real. I just saw Timmy. I can't believe it."

"You're good." Diane laughed as she attempted to clean up her face with a tissue while looking in the sun visor's mirror. "You should get an agent."

*   *   *

Jeremy was too freaked out by what had just happened to think about turning around and taking Diane home. Instead he just kept going on autopilot and drove to the Atco Cineplex. The radio filled in the silence between them as he drove. Once there, they had three choices for films that hadn't already started. The first was a romantic comedy staring an actress Jeremy detested, the second was a gross-out comedy that looked really funny in the commercials he had seen for it on television and the last was a serious Victorian-era drama that he would sooner amputate a limb than be forced to sit through.

Diane wanted to see the drama. Jeremy suggested seeing *School for Dudes.*

"Are you kidding?" Diane said. "It looks like the stupidest movie ever made from what I've seen of it. *Women and Whalebone* is getting great reviews. They say it's an Oscar contender."

They argued for a couple more minutes before they compromised and decided to see the romantic comedy neither of them wanted to go to. Another five minutes passed as Jeremy argued with the newly hired ticket seller, who wasn't aware that his familial connection with the theater's owner absolved him of paying for admission. Eventually another staff member noticed what was going on and informed the newcomer that Jeremy wasn't crazy, and that he was allowed to get his tickets without paying for them. Luckily the person behind the snack counter also recognized him, so he was able to get them their free snacks without any further trouble.

By the time they got to theater number six, the trailers were ending and the movie was about to begin. They could tell that the movie wasn't very popular because there was no one else in the theater except for a short, bearded fellow sitting alone in the back left-hand corner. They sat as far away from him as possible.

The movie started, and within a couple of minutes both had come to regret their compromise. But, because neither of them wanted to admit it, they stayed and endured the suffering in a silence that was broken only by the occasional guffaw that erupted from the odd man in the back.

Despite his better judgment, Jeremy actually found himself paying attention to the film's plot after a while, so he became annoyed when he started hearing a scratching sound behind him. It sounded like someone was loudly rubbing a hand against one of the theater's walls. Because there was only one other person in the theater with them, it was pretty obvious who was responsible for this distraction, but every time Jeremy turned in his seat to catch the weirdo in the act, the sound stopped and the guy acted as though he'd been sitting quietly in his seat the whole time. Eventually Jeremy lost his patience for this game, and he turned and shouted at the man. "Shut up!" he roared. "I didn't pay to listen to you scratch the freaking walls, you moron!"

The man appeared to be incredibly shocked by this outburst. He looked as though he was about to say something, but he thought better of it and decided to get up and leave instead.

"You didn't actually pay at all," Diane said when the man was gone.

"He didn't know that," he answered.

The two of them went back to watching the movie, and once again the lack of anything better to do compelled Jeremy to get involved with the story. He was actually coming close to being entertained when he started hearing the sound of a voice whispering behind him. He assumed it was the same man from before, who had returned to the theater just to annoy him some more, but when he turned around he saw that no one was there.

"Do you hear that?" he asked Diane.

"What?"

"Someone whispering behind us."

"That? That's just the sound of the movie playing in the theater next to us. The walls in these theaters aren't always as good at soundproofing as they should be."

Jeremy didn't argue, but he knew that his brother-in-law had spent a fortune soundproofing these walls, and not once during all of the movies he had seen at the Cineplex had he ever heard one while watching another.

The sound of the whispering continued and was soon joined by the sound of the occasional scratch along the wall. Jeremy started thinking he was going out of his mind when he remembered a conversation he had had with his brother-in-law during a recent family dinner at his parents' house.

"You're not going to believe this," Barry had said when they sat together watching a football game before the meal started, "but a bunch of my employees are saying that one of our theaters is haunted."

"Really?"

"Yeah, they say that people keep complaining about these strange sounds they hear in there while the movies are playing."

"What sort of sounds?"

"I dunno. Spooky sounds, I guess. Whispering voices and junk like that."

"Have you checked it out for yourself?"

"Nah, I don't believe in that crap."

"But if more than one person has heard these noises then there might be something to them," Jeremy said.

"Ah, they're all stoned. Trust me. There's a reason I make all of my money selling snacks."

At that point a commercial featuring an inordinately attractive young woman in a string bikini distracted them away from their conversation, and the subject was not brought up again. Jeremy had not thought about it again until this moment when he realized that he was currently sitting in the haunted movie theater.

"I don't believe it," he said aloud.

"What? That she would choose the bohemian poet over the stockbroker or that the bohemian poet lives in a loft whose rent would easily be at least six grand a month?" asked Diane, assuming he was talking about the movie.

"Two ghosts in one night!" Jeremy stood up from his seat and started pacing down the aisle. "I try to take a nice, attractive woman out on a date and not only does everything go wrong, but I also have to deal with two ghosts in one night!"

"What are you talking about?"

"This freaking theater is haunted! My brother-in-law told me about it a couple of weeks ago, but I forgot all about it. First I see that stupid half-deaf kid run out in front of me on the Burnt Mill Road, and now this! It's more than I can take!"

Diane spoke carefully. "Jeremy, are you supposed to be taking some kind of medication you didn't tell me about?"

"I'm not crazy!"

"Of course not, but I'm sure the pills help."

Jeremy yelled at her. "I don't take any pills!"

"Maybe you should."

"Look, I don't need advice from an animal psychic!"

"What's that supposed to mean?"

"It's not a real job!"

Diane glared at him. "Let me get this straight, the guy who is currently having a fit because of all the 'ghosts' he's encountered tonight has the nerve to tell me that I can't read animals' minds?"

"Yes! That is exactly what I am saying!"

"That's it," she said sharply. "I've had enough. I want you to take me home."

"With pleasure!"

The two of them then strode angrily out of the theater and made their way to Jeremy's car. Neither of them looked forward to having to spend another half-hour in each other's company.

"Worst date ever," Diane whispered to herself as Jeremy started his car.

"No argument here, honey," he answered back as he started driving.

"Marnie thinks you're a lousy employee," she told him cattily. "The only reason she keeps you around is because she likes how good you make her look to upper management."

"Yeah? Well the only reason I agreed to go out on this date was because she had begged me. She said I would be doing an act of charity by getting you out of the house after you got dumped by a circus clown!"

"He was not a circus clown. He was a juggler with the *Cirque du Soleil*, and I dumped him!"

"That's not what she said."

"She's a liar!"

"I'll tell her you called her that."

"You do and I'll destroy you!"

"How? Will you psychically command all of your animal friends to attack me?"

"No," she hissed at him. "I'll call my brother Tony and have him send a couple of our *family* friends to come over to your house and show you what your spine looks like!"

The two of them continued screaming at each other like that for the rest of the drive. They were midway along the Burnt Mill Road when Jeremy became so enraged that he turned from the wheel so he could wrap his hands around Diane's neck. Unfortunately for both of them, his elbow caught the wheel and caused it turn. Before they knew it, the car flew off the side of the rode into a very large tree. Neither of them had been wearing their seatbelts, and they both flew headfirst through the windshield.

Neither survived.

*   *   *

"And that," said Bobby, "is how the Burnt Mill Road came to be haunted by not just Timmy, but also Jeremy and Diane."

"What a strange story," said Suzie, his pretty, blond companion.

"It gets weirder," said Bobby, "because they say that if a man and a woman are driving along this road together on a chilly fall night like this—"

"It's summer. You've got the AC up on high."

"Right. Sorry, I'm just used to telling this story a certain way. What they say is that if a man and a woman are driving along this road together, regardless of the season or the present temperature, they can hear the ghosts of the two blind-daters fighting with each other on the side of the road if they roll down their windows and stay very quiet. Wanna try and hear them?"

"Okay."

They both rolled down their windows and listened intently to the sounds that whooshed by them as they drove.

"Can you hear anything?" he whispered.

"No," she whispered back.

He let a minute pass. "I think I hear them."

"Are you sure? I can't hear a thing."

"You have to really pay attention. You have to really concentrate, but you can definitely hear them."

She nodded silently and concentrated as hard as she possibly could on the sounds she was hearing outside.

HHHHHOOOOOONNNNNNNNKKKKK!!!!!!!!!!

Suzie jumped nearly a foot into the air with fright as Bobby started laughing with the kind of amusement that comes only when you have managed to reel your sucker in.

"You jerk!" She punched him in the arm. "I almost had a heart attack."

Bobby wiped the tears out of his eyes. "That one gets 'em every single time," he cackled. "It never fails!"

"You're freaking hilarious. That *Punk'd* guy has nothing on you, that's for sure."

"Oh, come on, don't be like that. You have to admit that was pretty funny."

"I don't have to admit anything, and you should pay attention while you're driving. There's a kid up ahead standing in the middle of the road."

"No, there isn't."

"What are talking about? Can't you see him?"

"I don't see nothing, but—OHMYGOD!"

Bobby swerved to avoid hitting the boy, but he was too late.

At that point there should have been a thump, but instead the two of them watched as the car drove straight through the boy, as if he wasn't even there.

"Did you—" Bobby attempted to ask.

Suzie nodded.

"That was—"

She nodded again.

"Uh, I don't think I'm up for seeing a movie tonight," Bobby said. "Why don't we just turn around and stop in at a bar instead?"

"Yeah, that sounds good to me."

Burlington

Vernon Green woke up with a tremendous headache. As he started to sit up, he was shocked to discover that chains, leading to a single padlock in the middle of the cold, dark cell, were shackled to his hands and feet.

"They put me in the dungeon," he said to himself as he realized what was going on. "What did I do?" he wondered aloud.

The "dungeon" was the name used by everyone at the Burlington County Prison to describe cell number five. Located in the center of the third floor, it was the prison's maximum security cell, designed to hold the most violent and dangerous of offenders. Unlike the other cells, it did not have a fireplace—which made it very cold during the winter—and it was situated so that whoever was inside it could be kept under constant supervision.

Until two days ago, it had been the home of Joseph Clough, who had lived there for a year until his death sentence was finally carried out. Unlike Clough, Vernon was not a murderer, nor had he been sentenced to death for the bank robbery that had led to his incarceration in the first place, so it was odd that he would find himself shivering in chains in the prison's most infamous room.

Then he remembered the remark he had made about the keeper's lovely young wife, and his situation suddenly made a lot of sense.

He couldn't help it. She was so pretty and so feminine that it was impossible for him not to comment on her attributes during breakfast the week before. Unfortunately, the keeper overheard what he had said, and his current situation was the result.

Burlington County Prison entrance

There were still another 10 years left on his sentence, and Vernon worried he might spend a decade rotting in the dungeon. He quickly eased his mind by convincing himself that it was only a matter of time before a truly violent criminal was sentenced to Burlington, and the keeper would be forced to send him back to a regular cell.

His head still throbbing, he heard his chains rattle as he lifted his arm and touched the back of his head. There he found a large bump, which he assumed was the result of the blow the guards had inflicted on him to get him into the dungeon as quickly and quietly as possible.

"Bastards," Vernon muttered to himself. "Bastards!" He shouted it this time so the guards could hear him. His chains rattled as he further illustrated his displeasure with an obscene gesture, which, given the design of the cell, he knew they could all see.

BANG! The sound of a truncheon slamming against his cell door got his attention, and he froze in place.

"You best be quiet in there, Green," sneered Johnson, the third floor's head guard. "Keeper Willis is still mighty riled over what you said about his missus, so if you know what's good for you, you'll not say a peep until someone else angers him and takes your place."

It was good advice, and Vernon decided to heed it.

*   *   *

Completed in 1811, Burlington County Prison was an intimidating building crafted out of brick, stone and concrete, with a massive front door, vaulted ceilings and cold, whitewashed walls. It was designed to hold 40 prisoners, many of whom lived their last days in the prison, thanks to a New Jersey state law that mandated that all criminals convicted of capital crimes be executed in the counties in which they were tried. For nearly 100 years the people of Burlington County were able to attend the public hangings that ended many a criminal's stay.

The most famous of these executed lawbreakers was a murderer named Joseph Clough. Clough was a cruel, superstitious man who enjoyed hurting people but who had a tremendous fear of the supernatural. A paranoid man, he believed that everywhere he went he was in danger of being killed by a vampire or a werewolf.

For several years Clough had kept a mistress. June was a petite, pretty woman who was 20 years his junior. He took her for granted and often treated her with contempt, but he also paid her rent and her bills, so she put up with his abuse. That is, until the day she met a man her age who treated her with great kindness and who was willing to make her an honest woman. She agreed to marry the man, but she knew that Clough would not take kindly to the idea of her no longer being at his ready disposal.

Unfortunately for her, she chose the worst possible night to tell him.

It was a dark, rainy night—exactly the kind that aroused Clough's worst fears. It was the kind of weather that he imagined attracted the worst kind of spooks and demons. On his way home when the storm started, he decided instead to seek refuge at his mistress' house and wait there until the storm abated.

She was surprised to see him but let him in, deciding this was a good opportunity to tell him about her important news: she was moving away from Burlington to live with her future husband in Hackensack. She didn't notice the strange look in his eyes. If she had, she might have known to bite her tongue and inform him of her upcoming departure with a note instead.

"Joseph," she said, as she poured him a drink. "I have something I have to tell you."

"Do you now?" he responded, looking over his shoulder to see if he could spot any foul creatures lurking outside her living room window.

"I want you to know that I appreciate all that you've done for me over the years. I had nothing when you found me, and you helped me find someplace to live and gave me money for food and clothes. If it weren't for you I don't know where I would be right now, but—"

She turned and saw that he was eyeing her suspiciously.

"I found you in that tavern, just outside of Camden," he said in a voice that made her feel very uncomfortable. "You said you had no family."

"That's right, and—"

"And I was foolish enough to believe you, wasn't I?"

"What are you saying?"

"You think I wouldn't figure it out!" he roared at her. "You're no woman, you're a vile succubus! For years now you've been sucking the life out of me so you could keep living your foul life!"

"Joseph, I don't understand—" She tried to protest, but it was too late. He got up and hit her so hard she fell onto a nearby table, causing it to break apart.

He bent down and picked up one of the table's splintered legs.

"I know how to deal with your kind," he told her.

June screamed as he held the table leg above his head. Her screaming stopped when he brought it down.

Days later he was arrested for her murder and sentenced to hang. He was sent to Burlington County Prison and immediately placed into cell number five, where he was kept in chains and placed on constant supervision. There he ranted and screamed at his captors, accusing them of being the foulest kinds of beasts. His madness had so overtaken him that he now could see only monsters around him and no longer had any contact with the world of men. The guards were much relieved when in 1855—after a year in the dungeon—it finally came time to carry out his sentence.

They dragged him screaming out of the cell.

"I curse you demons," he swore at them. "I curse you all! You think you've beaten me, but my soul is not so easily taken! Do what you will to my body—I'll be back! I'll be back to torment you until the end of time! Mark my words!"

It took the pull of the noose on his neck to finally silence his oath of revenge on the prison and the men who kept him in chains, but he did not stay quiet for long.

*   *   *

Vernon had barely been in the dungeon for one whole day when he realized his situation was even more dire than he had first imagined it. It was sometime during the

"Get me out of here!" Vernon cried.

middle of the night—he didn't have access to a timepiece, so he did not know the exact hour—when he started hearing the sound of a voice whispering frantically from a point somewhere close to him. The words were spoken so quickly they streamed into one long sound, but he was still somehow able to understand what they were.

"*Curseyou,youfoul,loathsomedemons,curseyoutohell. Ishallberevenged,Ishallberevenged*" was what the voice kept repeating over and over again.

It took Vernon no time at all to figure out the cause of this strange phenomenon. "It's Clough!" he stood up and shrieked at the top of his lungs. "He's in here with me! Get me out of here! Get me out of here!"

BANG! This time the sound of Johnson's truncheon on the door wasn't enough to silence Vernon's cries.

"Get me out of here!" he continued. "It's Clough! He's in here with me!"

"If you don't shut up, Green, we'll have to come in there and do it for you," threatened Johnson, but Vernon didn't hear him. He kept screaming and stopped only when a blow to the back of his head dropped him to the floor.

Johnson knew instantly that something was wrong. He had only meant to get the fool to stop screaming, but he had misjudged the force of his blow and had killed the prisoner. Acting quickly, he gathered some other guards. They quickly dug a shallow grave in the prison's cemetery and buried Vernon's body just before sunrise.

When the keeper asked what had happened to the prisoner he had sent to the dungeon, he was told that the man had started making noises in the middle of the night and that when Johnson went in to see what was wrong, Green was already dead.

"It must have been his heart," Johnson told Willis. "That's how my father went. He was perfectly healthy one day, and he dropped dead the next."

Willis thought this explanation sounded reasonable and did not look into the matter any further. A new, more deserving criminal was moved into cell number five. And, before his first night was through, the prisoner complained loudly to Johnson that he would never be able to sleep as long as "these two goddamn voices keep whisperin' at me!"

The Little Devils
Part II:
Rachel Letton's
British Soldier

"And that," said Danny as he finished reading the story, "is how the Jersey Devil came to be!"

"No, it's not," said Max.

"Yes it is," Donny argued back. "It says right here in this book!"

"Then that book is wrong, because this book has a completely different explanation for the Jersey Devil's origin."

"And what does it say?" asked Andy.

Max picked up the book he had been reading and starting telling them the really true legend of the Jersey Devil.

*   *   *

Rachel Letton was a minister's daughter, a role she took very seriously. In accordance with her father's wishes, she studied the Bible every day and avoided the company of boys and any person who did not follow the path of righteousness. The boys of Leeds Point were not keen on her religious devotion because she was easily the prettiest girl in town, and they all desperately wanted to spend some time in her company.

But the only boy her father allowed to be with her unattended was a blind orphan named Colin. Her father had taken the boy in when he was 13 and had raised him like a son. He thought nothing of leaving the boy with his daughter, assuming that Colin's blindness would not allow him to appreciate Rachel's beauty. He was wrong. Not being able to see Rachel did not stop Colin from falling in love with her.

If she knew of his romantic adoration toward her, she did not show it. Most likely she interpreted his kindness as merely familial devotion. After all they were—by law, if not by blood—technically brother and sister.

His love for her was such that he was even more vigilant than their father in making sure that Rachel would spend no time alone with any boy. He knew it was only a matter of time before one of them would come and take her away from him, but he was determined to make sure that this was a long time in coming.

The family was so devoted to their duties to their church that they were barely aware of the war that was looming over the horizon. Minister Letton's only loyalty was to God, and he had yet to decide whether he supported the King of England or his fellow colonists. His children thought so highly of him that they held off forming their own opinions until he had told them what he had decided.

When it became clear the war was inevitable and he had to choose a side, the minister prayed on the matter. When he finished, he told Rachel and Colin that he had decided that he would support the colonists. They both agreed to do the same, but—though she would never admit it—Rachel had secretly hoped he'd come to the other conclusion. Her late mother had instilled in her a deep respect for her heritage and for the royal family that led the country of her ancestry, and she was not completely comfortable with the thought of turning her back on that part of her life forever.

The three of them were soon lending aid to the rebel cause, though the minister and Colin were both leery of how this aid required that Rachel spend much of her time with grown men, all of whom were captivated by her charms.

Rachel, for her part, found herself thinking thoughts she had never considered before. So many of the young soldiers she aided in the course of her duties were strong and handsome, and they flirted with her in a manner to which she was not accustomed. She tried her best to repulse this kind of attention and keep all of her interactions as businesslike as possible, but she found that a large part of her was actually enjoying this newfound attention.

As she lay in her bed at night, she found herself thinking more and more about how much she wanted to know what love was like—what it felt like to be held and, most importantly, what it felt like to be kissed.

Soon these thoughts were invading her daydreams as well, and she was deep in thought while retrieving water from the well behind their home. Rachel was lifting up a full bucket when she heard the sound of something struggling in the forest behind her. At first she thought it was an animal, but by the amount of noise it made she quickly gathered that it had to be a man.

"Hello?" she shouted out into the forest, unsure if she wanted an answer.

"Please," a strained voice said. "I need some help."

She moved quickly toward the voice and gasped when she saw a British soldier lying on the ground. "What happened to you?" she asked him.

"Shot," he struggled to say. "My men and I were caught in an ambush. They're all dead, but I managed to make it out alive."

Although he was her enemy, Rachel felt pity for the man at her feet. Looking at him, she knew that God would not want her to forsake the man simply for fighting against the side her father had chosen, so she helped him to his feet and supported him as they moved toward the house.

"Where are you taking me?" he asked, his voice barely breaking above a whisper.

"Somewhere safe," she said, knowing there was only one place where she could tend to his wounds without arousing suspicion.

When her mother died, her passing had been so sudden and painful that no one in the family was prepared to deal with it. Since then her room had become something of a shrine that no one dared enter. It had been five years since its door had last been opened—a fact confirmed by the thick layer of dust that covered everything inside the room.

Rachel led him into the room and gently placed him on her mother's bed. "It's very gothic," he said jokingly.

"I'm sorry about all of the dust. It's been a very long time since we've had any use for this room."

She waited for the soldier to respond, but he was so exhausted that he had already fallen into a deep sleep. Rachel checked his wound. She was far from being an expert, but she knew enough to determine that though it must have been very painful, it was not at all life threatening. As long as she could keep infection from setting in, the soldier in her mother's bed would live to see another day.

She let him sleep as she cleaned and dressed his wound as carefully as she could. When she was finished she realized she would have to leave right away or else her father or brother would start wondering where she was, but before she could go she had to tell the soldier some very important information. She gently shook him until he finally awoke.

"So it is true," he said after he opened his eyes. "I was afraid I was still outside and dreaming that I had been rescued by a very pretty girl."

She shushed him with her index finger raised to her lips. "If you're going to stay here, you have to stay as quiet as you possibly can. If anyone hears a sound coming out of this room, they'll immediately investigate. Then the wound you have now will be the least of your concerns."

"I understand. I'll be as quiet as the moon in the sky."

"I have to go now," said Rachel, "but I'll be back as soon as I can manage it. I've left you some water and some food if you feel strong enough to eat and drink while I'm gone."

"Your kindness is overwhelming," he whispered.

Rachel blushed and excused herself from the room. She found Colin and her father sitting in the kitchen.

"Where were you, my child?" asked her father. "We were about to send out a search party to find you."

"I was doing some sewing and completely lost track of all sense of time. You two must be starving. How does some nice hot stew sound?"

"Like a gift from heaven," answered her father.

"What were you sewing?" asked Colin.

"Uh," she said hesitantly, not used to lying. "I was stitching up an old dress of Mother's I found. With some small repairs it'll be as good as new, and you know how hard finding nice clothing is these days."

"And what's the occasion that demands such a fine outfit?" asked her adopted brother.

Rachel laughed. "Colin, a lady doesn't need a specific occasion to justify wanting a nice dress to wear."

That answer seemed to mollify him, and she went to work making their supper.

As was their habit, her father and her brother left for their rooms after they had finished eating. With them gone, she rushed back to her mother's old room and found the soldier sleeping soundly.

"*Thank heaven he's not a snorer,*" she thought as she checked his bandage.

She heard him whisper as she was inspecting the quality of her work. "I was dreaming about you, and I realized I don't even know your name."

"It's Rachel."

"That's a beautiful name. It's much better than mine."

"Which is?"

"Herbert," he answered with a frown.

Rachel stifled her impulse to laugh.

"I know. My parents weren't very thoughtful when it came time to name me."

"Herbert is perfectly fine name." Rachel lied yet again, something she had done more of in the past couple of hours than she had over the course of her life up to that point.

Herbert smiled. "No, it isn't, but thank you for saying so."

They had to decide whether to support the King of England or the colonists.

"How are you feeling?

"Dizzy, a bit nauseous. Mostly I feel grateful that you found me when you did and chose not to leave me to die."

"It was nothing," she said. "Any decent Christian would have done the same."

"I would not be surprised if it was a decent Christian who shot me," he answered. "Most people would not have done what you did, Rachel. You are an extraordinary person. My guardian angel."

Rachel felt the warmth in her face as blood raced to her cheeks and she blushed with delight. "You must get some more sleep. I'll leave you be."

"Please don't," he said. "I feel so much better whenever you're in the room with me."

"But—"

"Please."

Rachel relented and pulled a nearby chair up to the bed and sat down beside him. He reached out and took her hand and held it. It was the most intimate experience of her life to that point. They just sat there and stared at each other, waiting for the morning to come, when she would have to leave him alone again.

But she did not want to go. She wanted to do something else instead.

With his permission, she did.

*   *   *

"What did she do?" asked Donny.

"I dunno," admitted Max as he looked up from the book he was reading from. "It just says they did something. Maybe they kissed?"

"Well then why doesn't the book just say that they kissed?" Donny protested.

Andy spoke up. "Maybe they—y'know…"

"What?" asked Max.

Andy started to blush. *"Y'know,* more than kissing…"

"You don't mean…" Donny looked over his shoulder to make sure his mom wasn't within a mile of him, "S-E-X?" he spelled the word out.

Andy nodded. "Maybe Herbert hit a home run."

"I don't think they had baseball back then," said Donny.

"You know what I mean," Andy sighed.

"But how?" asked Max. "He was wounded. Wouldn't he have been in pain the whole time?"

"How hurt would you have to be to tell Tina DeMarco that you wouldn't go to home base with her?" asked Andy.

Max considered this for a moment. "I get your point."

*   *   *

Colin didn't have to see to notice that Rachel was behaving oddly. Their father may have been too wrapped in other concerns to notice, but, when it came to Rachel, Colin could not be distracted. With only his ears as his guide, he started keeping track of her activities and noticed that she kept disappearing for minutes, sometimes hours, at a time. It didn't take a detective to deduce that finding out where she was during these moments was the key to unlocking the reasons behind her strange behavior. Unfortunately, it was nearly impossible to follow her undetected without being able to see her. No, if he wanted to find out where she was going, he would need someone else's help. Not wanting to get his father involved, he would have to go to someone outside of the family, which left him with few available choices.

"I'm not sure I understand," Sophie admitted after hearing Colin's scheme. "You're going to hire me to do housework, but you want me to spend my time following your sister?"

"That's right."

"Why?"

"I'm not sure yet. I know she's up to something, but I'm in no position to find out what that is myself."

Sophie was the 15-year-old daughter of Sam Wishbane, the local blacksmith. Despite his profession, Sam truly respected a good education and had come to feel greatly ashamed of his own illiteracy. He had decided when his daughter turned eight that she would learn how to read and write. He had sent Sophie to Minister Letton, who handed her over to Rachel, who tutored the child until she was 12 and literate enough for her father's satisfaction. Since then Sophie had made it her habit to visit the Lettons at least once a week, which made her Colin's best choice for a potential aide in his mission to uncover Rachel's secret. He could tell his father and Rachel that the Wishbanes were doing poorly, so he had hired Sophie to help around the house. No one would suspect the real purpose of her being there.

"All right," Sophie said. "We could use the money."

"Good girl," Colin replied, smiling.

If Rachel thought it was odd that Colin had hired her former student to help around the house, her voice did not show it. She seemed to accept the news without question, before—once again—disappearing for an hour.

Although she had agreed to take the job, Sophie was somewhat reluctant to fulfill her main duty. She had grown to consider Rachel a good friend during the time she spent as her student and felt bad about spying on her, especially if it turns out that the reason for her mysterious behavior was something that was really no one's business but her own. Still, she had taken the money and felt she had to earn it, so she kept a vigilant eye on the minister's daughter.

Rachel, for her part, was not fooled by Colin's deception. She knew right from the start why Sophie had suddenly appeared in their home as a housekeeper, but there was little she could do about it. Herbert was not well enough to be moved, and even if he was, she had nowhere else to take him. Over the past week she tried to insulate her mother's room with sheets, rags and anything else that she thought might muffle the sound of their voices, and her efforts seemed to have been worth it. During a rare moment when only she and Herbert remained in the house, she stood outside the door as he spoke at a normal volume; she couldn't hear a word of what he was saying. She was certain that as long as they kept whispering, there was no way for them to be detected by sound.

After Sophie's arrival Rachel carefully watched her watcher, taking note of every moment Sophie's eyes were upon her. A week passed, and Sophie had little to report to Colin—from what she could see, Rachel's activities were not at all out of the ordinary.

"She must be on to you," Colin explained. "You're going to have be less obvious. Figure out ways to spy on her without her knowing that you're around."

"But how am I supposed to do that?" Sophie asked.

"You're a clever girl, figure that out for yourself."

Sophie was a clever girl, but espionage had never been a subject to which she had given any thought. Still, she was getting paid, so she decided to do several things that she figured might help her cause. First, she practiced being as quiet she could, seeing how long she could go, both moving and still, without making a sound. Then she studied the house in an attempt to find every available hiding spot. And it was during this part of her studies that she made the odd discovery that there was a door in the house that was always locked.

"That was Mother's room, before she died," Colin told her when she asked him about it. "Do you think it could have something to do with what Rachel is up to?"

"It makes sense to me," Sophie said. "Do you have a key I can use to get inside the room?"

"No, but I can get one from my father," he told her.

Sophie went back to her "work" while Colin went off to find his father and ask for the key.

He returned a half-hour later with a sour expression on his face. "Rachel is a smart one, there's no doubt of that," he told Sophie.

"What did she do?"

"The key is gone. She had gotten to it first."

"Is that door the only way to get into that room?"

Colin thought for a moment before a large smile broke out across his face. "Sophie, you really are a bright one, aren't you? I know for a fact that in the kitchen there is a dumbwaiter that goes up to that room. We used it when our mother could no longer get out of bed."

The two of them went over to the kitchen, and Sophie examined the dumbwaiter.

"So?" asked Colin. "Is it big enough for you to fit in?

"I suppose," Sophie admitted, not particularly looking forward to the idea of being trapped inside that thing as it ascended the floors of the house.

"Then get in! There's no time like the present," he told her excitedly.

She squeezed her way into the contraption and felt it rise as Colin started pulling on the rope. Thankfully the trip was a short one, and only a minute had passed before she reached the room. With a sigh of relief she opened the small door and carefully extricated herself from the dumbwaiter, taking care to be as quiet as possible. When she was completely out, she turned around and saw that she was protected by a dressing shade that had been stuck in front of the food elevator.

"Did you hear something?" Sophie heard a voice whisper from behind the shade.

"Are you still so paranoid after all this time?" whispered someone else.

"Time has not made our situation any less precarious," explained the first voice. "If we are caught, the consequences will be the same now as they were in the beginning."

"I suppose you are right, and no, I did not hear a noise."

Sophie recognized one of the voices as Rachel's, but she could not identify the other. She looked around the small area she found herself in for a way to see the rest of the room without being detected, but there were no convenient eyeholes anywhere. Instead all she found was a suit folded at her feet. She bent over and examined it and almost gasped aloud when she realized it was the uniform of a British solider.

This was Rachel's secret, and the thought of it almost caused Sophie to hyperventilate. But before that happened, she calmed herself down and slowly and quietly climbed back into the dumbwaiter. Colin lowered her down and asked her what she had found.

"Nothing," Sophie said hesitantly.

Although Colin could not see her face, he could still tell that she was lying to him. "What is in there, Sophie? You have to tell me!"

Tears flooded out of Sophie's eyes as she told Colin what she had seen and heard inside the locked room.

Colin went pale. He knew what it could mean to the family if a secret like this got out. Seen as being sympathizers to the Crown and enemies of the Revolution, they would be driven from their home, which would then most probably be burned to the ground. "You can't tell anyone else about this. No one! Do you understand?"

"Yes sir," Sophie answered, her voice breaking from the stress of the situation.

He pulled out his change purse and handed her the money he had promised her. "Now go," he told her. "Go home and never speak to anyone of this ever again."

Sophie took the money and ran out of the house. Colin had no idea if he could trust her, but he assumed that he would soon find out. He rushed as quickly as he could to his adoptive mother's old room and banged on the door as loudly as he could.

"Open up, Rachel!" "I know who's in there. I know what you're hiding. We have to get him out of here before anyone else finds out about it."

For a moment nothing seemed to happen, but then he heard the sound of the door opening.

"How—" Rachel started to ask, but he had no time to explain.

"Never mind how," he interrupted. "If the townspeople find out that we have been giving aid and shelter to a wounded British soldier, it will be our doom. We have to get him out of here."

"But where?" she protested. "There is nowhere to take him!"

"It does not matter where. For our sakes we have to just dump him back into the woods and let him fend for himself!"

"But we can't do that!"

"We're at war, Rachel!"

"You don't understand!"

"You love him? Is that it? Well, is your love worth the destruction of your entire family? Is it worth tarnishing our reputation and having us forever being branded as traitors?" As his tirade caused his sister to break down into a river of tears, Colin heard a stranger's voice speak.

"There's more to it than that."

"What?" said Colin, who realized he was speaking to the man he had just suggested be dumped unmercifully into the woods and left to his own devices.

"She's carrying my child," answered the soldier.

At that moment, Colin's heart and mind exploded. "She's…what?" he spoke, his mind racing so fast his thoughts no longer made any kind of rational sense.

"It's true," Rachel told him. "I'm pregnant with his child. I *do* love him, but that alone is not the only reason why I cannot abandon him to die. But if it means saving you and our father from harm, I shall leave with him and we shall do our best to survive on our own."

"No," Colin shook his head. "Stay here. I'll try and think of a way out of this."

He left the two of them alone to think of a solution to this horrible predicament. He was so shocked by the news that Rachel was with child that everything else now seemed so trivial and unimportant. A large part of him felt completely betrayed by her actions, but he could not bear the thought of what might happen to her if he banished her and her British soldier from their home. He had to think—there *had* to be a way out of this.

But before a solution came, he heard the sound of a rumbling mob approaching their home. Sophie had not been able to keep her secret. It was too late to do anything.

"What is that racket?" he heard his father ask.

Colin could not bear to tell his father the whole truth, so he shared with him only a small part of it. "They think we're nursing a wounded British soldier in our home," he told him.

"But that's preposterous! How could they believe such a ridiculous notion?"

Colin lied. "I don't know."

"Well, I'll certainly put a stop to this," said the minister as he walked to the front door.

"Father," Colin said, "I don't think that's a good idea."

"Nonsense. They won't hurt me. I've known most of them for their entire lives," he said as he opened the door.

Before he could speak he was pelted by a hail of rocks, thrown at him by the angry mob.

"Traitorous scum!" shouted Sam Wishbane, who had organized the mob after his daughter told him what she had seen inside the Letton home.

The minister tried to defend himself, but the crowd refused to hear his pleas. When one of the rocks hit his temple, he collapsed to the ground—dead.

Colin's blindness prevented him from seeing what the senseless mob had done, but he knew it would not be safe for him to confront the crowd with any kind of rational argument. All they wanted now was blood, and they would not stop until they had had their fill.

"Rachel!" he called out to his sister. "We must go now! Out the back way! It's our only hope!"

Before he could say anything else, a rock hit Colin squarely in the back of his head. He fell to the ground in an unconscious heap, and the mob behind him trampled his prone body as everyone stormed inside the home and started to set it ablaze.

Rachel and Herbert struggled to get out through the back door. Herbert was still too injured to walk on his own, and Rachel could barely bear the burden of his weight as she tried to keep him on his feet.

"Leave me behind," Herbert said. "They're out for blood, and I couldn't bear to see what they would do to you."

Rachel encouraged him. "No, we can make it."

"No, we can't. Not together. You have to drop me here and run—as fast as you can and without looking back."

"I can't—"

"I'm not asking you, Rachel," Herbert stated, grimacing through his pain. "This is not a request. If you stay, you will die, and I will not be the cause of that. As proof of his words, Herbert pushed himself away from her and collapsed to the ground. "Run!" he screamed at her as she attempted to get him back to his feet. "If you really do love me—if you have ever loved me—you'll run and leave me here! Do it! Now!"

Tears streaming down her face, Rachel let go of her lover and the father of her unborn child and did as she was told. She ran as fast as her feet could carry her. She did not look back.

If she had, she would have seen what the mob did to the man she loved, and the sight of it would have killed her where she stood.

She made it into the forest and stopped only when her legs and lungs would not allow her to move another inch. She fell to her knees and began to sob. For the first time in her life, Rachel Letton knew what it was like to feel hate. It burned inside her and caused her to curse those who had done this to her. "They will know no peace," she cried. "They will know no safety! As long as they and each generation that follows them exists, they will know the terror and pain they caused me this day!"

These were the last words she spoke before she lay down on the ground. Her heart broken and her body exhausted, she could think of no reason to get up, and she stayed in that spot until she died.

The story should have ended there, but someone—or something—was listening when she spoke her last words. The curse would not go unfulfilled. Although Rachel was dead, the tiny new life inside her carried on. As the months passed it grew into something that bore little resemblance to its human ancestry—something monstrous, something almost demonic. It stayed inside Rachel's decomposing body until finally all of her flesh had rotted away.

Free at last, the horrible creature escaped into the forest and started on the mission its mother had given it with her very last words—it searched out the people responsible for her misery and death and made sure that they never again knew a moment's peace or safety...

To Be Continued

The Hookerman

Lester Clemmons had a very lonely job. He worked for the railroad and spent his days traveling down the tracks in New Jersey's Budd Lake area, looking for potential problems and making any necessary repairs. He longed to have a partner to join him on his rounds, but his bosses felt that it was a one-man job and that there was no point in incurring the expense of hiring an additional worker. It was because of his loneliness that Lester took to talking to himself. As he worked he would engage himself in long conversations about politics, the weather and current events, always taking care to give equal time to both sides of the argument so that one was never less represented than the other.

Lester was crazy.

Whether the result of the enforced solitude of his labors or a natural predisposition toward insanity, Lester's mind had sailed long ago past the point where he could reasonably determine fantasy from reality. But such was the nature of his mental illness that very few of the people who knew him had any idea that he was no longer at the controls of his own inner engine.

Still, a firm grasp of reality was not especially necessary when it came to repairing train tracks, so it really didn't matter if Lester was sane or not—that is, until the day he managed to argue himself into the situation that ended his life.

It all started as he attempted to catch some sleep on the small cot that sat in the corner of the rickety shack he called home. The trouble was that a part of his brain kept insisting he get up and check a potential problem he had spotted along the tracks that afternoon. He hadn't had the proper tools with him to fix it, so he had decided to return to it the next day, but now his more anxious half was concerned that the problem couldn't wait.

"Do you want to be responsible for a train crash?" he asked the half of him that just wanted to sleep. "Could you really handle having that on your conscience?"

He yawned and answered himself by making two salient points. "First off, there's no way that a couple of loose ties are going to derail a train, and even if they could, there's no train scheduled to go down those tracks until tomorrow night."

"Anything can happen," his other voice argued, "and schedules have been known to change."

"I don't care," he insisted. "I've just got comfortable and nothing you say can get me up until tomorrow morning."

*   *   *

Lester muttered several obscenities to himself as he rode his bike to the pertinent ties. Controlling the bike was proving quite difficult, because his balance was affected by both the heavy pack of tools that was strapped to his back and the lantern he held aloft with his right hand. The moon was nowhere in sight, thanks to the dark storm clouds that littered the night sky, and even with the lantern it was hard to find his way in the dark. A few times along the way he ran into obstructions that caused him to fly off the bike and onto the cold ground below.

Then it started to rain.

It was too late for Lester to turn back and go home. He was nearly there and—now that he had the proper tools—it would take him just a few minutes to fix the problem and set his mind at ease, so he carried on as thunder roared following the quick bursts of lightning he saw in the distance.

He finally made it to the site of the two loose ties. Unfortunately, in the dark it was difficult to determine exactly which ties those two were, even with the help of the lamp he was carrying. Lester grumbled as he started testing every single tie until he finally found the two he had come all this way to repair. Now that he was back he realized that they really weren't that loose, and he could have easily waited until the morning to fix them, but because he was already there he just sighed and started going to work.

First he had to pry loose the old spikes that were keeping the ties in place. The weather had caused them to rust, and they were no longer the right size and shape to keep the ties as steady as they should be. But rusted or not, they were still stuck hard in the ties, and getting them out took a lot of muscle. He set his lamp at his feet and started grunting and groaning as he worked to pry the first spike out of its tie.

After 15 minutes of very hard work he was able to at last pull the spike out of the tie and throw it down at his feet. He now had just three more to go.

"You should have stayed in bed," said the more rational part of his mind.

"He's right; you should have," his more anxious side agreed.

"Too late now," he muttered to both of them.

As was his custom, Lester tried to take his mind off of his hard work by engaging himself in a conversation. The newspapers at the time were all full of the news that President Garfield, who had been shot in July by that madman Guiteau, had been taken to the seaside town of Elberon, where Lester's sister lived.

"Best thing to happen to New Jersey!" his rational side declared out loud. "Once he gets better, everyone will come here to recuperate by the sea!"

"Nonsense," disagreed his anxious half. "He's a sure goner, and once he dies no one is going to want to visit the town where the president snuffed it."

"Sure they would," he said. "For the history and what-not."

"History? Who cares about history these days! All any-body cares about now is the present. I blame the steam engine. It's made life speed by too fast. Now, what used to take months or even years can be accomplished in just a few weeks. They say it's progress, but the reality is that now no one has time to think about anything other than the immediate future. It won't last, I tell you. People can only take so much. Soon they're going to get tired and insist we return to a less fast-paced mode of life."

"How can you say that?" he asked himself. "Without the steam engine, you wouldn't have a job. The progress you complain about puts food on your table and gives you a roof above your head."

"It also forces me to spend time with a fool like you," he complained as he managed to get the second spike out.

Lester argued with himself like this for another half hour as he worked on the spikes in the second tie. Finally he was finished that part of the job, and it was now time to hammer in the new spikes.

"You better rest, Lester," he told himself, "or else you won't be able to lift your arms tomorrow."

It was true that his arms were sore, but Lester ignored himself; he wanted to get back to bed as soon as he could, so he started hammering in the spikes as fast as he could. The first two he got in fairly easily, but by the time he started working on the third, his arms were so sore that he could barely lift his hammer from the ground, much less above his head.

"Dammit," he swore, realizing he was going to have to wait until his strength returned. Having nothing better to do, he sat down and started arguing with himself about whether or not brown eggs tasted any different than white eggs.

The argument might have continued for quite some time, but he was so tired that he started to fall asleep. He tried to fight it, but eventually his eyelids grew too heavy, and he slumped further down on the ground.

He would have slept there all night were it not for the sudden sense of vibration that awoke him. It was still dark out, but from the sound he was hearing and the sensation he was feeling, it was obvious that the schedule had changed and a train was on its way. Knowing he had to move or else risk being squashed by the oncoming locomotive, he tried to stand up, but discovered that something was keeping him from moving. His arm appeared to have become wedged within the space between the inside and outside rails. He tried to pull it out, but it would not budge.

The sound of the approaching train grew louder with each second. Lester became more and more desperate as he attempted to extricate himself from his predicament. With his free hand he lifted up his still-burning lamp. He could not yet see the train, which meant he had a few minutes left before it was too late.

The moon was nowhere in sight, thanks to the dark storm clouds that littered the night sky.

It soon became clear that there was no way he was going to be able to pull his arm out of the space it was wedged in without someone else's help. His heart started to race as he realized he was now only moments away from his certain death.

"Wait!" his less rational voice shouted out. "What do animals do when they get caught in traps like this?"

"You can't mean—" he couldn't believe what he was suggesting.

"It's our only hope!" he insisted.

With great disbelief, he set down his lantern, reached over to his satchel of tools and searched with his hand for the saw he always carried with him.

"Hurry!" he shouted at himself. "There's no time!"

He grabbed the saw and gritted his teeth as he pressed it against his own arm and started sawing back and forth as fast as he could. He felt surprisingly little pain. His instinct to live was so strong that it managed to block out anything that would keep him from doing what he had to do. He looked up from his work and saw the train in the distance. He managed to saw even faster and was now nearly halfway through the bone.

It was at that point that the pain came, and it came hard. Lester began to scream, but as loud as that scream was, it was no match for the roar of the oncoming engine that was getting closer and closer with each movement of the saw in his hand.

"You can do it, you crazy old fool," he urged himself through his gritted teeth. "Just a bit more…"

The train was almost upon him, and he had cut all the way through the bone—all that was left was the remainder of his flesh. He pumped the blade as fast as his exhausted arm could move it, and—at last—he was free from his trap. He rolled away to safety just as the speeding train whooshed past him with a force that would have pulverized him had he not gotten out of the way in time.

Somehow he managed to stagger to his feet and began moving to get some help, but he was losing far too much blood. As amazing as his escape was, it was all for naught; his legs gave out from under him, and he collapsed on the ground and bled to death.

*   *   *

Bruce and his friends were on their way to getting very wasted. The keg they had been drinking from was nearly tapped out, which meant it was time to move on to the harder stuff. Someone pulled out a bottle of peach schnapps, and it made its way around the circle they had formed around the campfire.

"Someone tell us a ghost story," suggested Molly, whose eyes were obviously bleary from the alcohol.

"Yeah," agreed a chorus of slurred voices.

"You guys want a ghost story?" asked Bruce, who sounded deceptively sober compared to his friends.

"Yes!" they answered him all together.

"How many of you have heard the story of the Hookerman?" he asked.

No one said a word. A hush fell over them as Bruce prepared to tell them the tale.

"They say that his spirit haunts the train tracks that run just a few miles from here. Years ago he was the guy who took care of those tracks, but one night he got his arm caught while he was making a repair, and the only way for him to avoid being hit by a train was to cut off his own arm—"

"Euwwwwww," groaned several of the more sensitive souls sitting around the fire.

Bruce continued. "They found him dead in a field a quarter of a mile away from the tracks. He had managed to walk that far before he bled to death. Ever since then, his spirit keeps coming back to the tracks to search for the arm he left behind. You can tell he's there because you can see the glow of the lamp he had been using that night floating in the air as he looks for his severed limb. Pretty wicked, huh?"

His friend Gary answered by blowing a raspberry. "That's freakin' ridiculous," he added immediately afterward. "That never happened."

"Sure it did," said Bruce. "Do you want me to prove it to you guys?"

Everyone agreed this sounded like a fine idea.

"Then let's head over to the tracks and catch sight of some of that Hookerman action," he said as he stood up.

Everyone followed his lead and got up and headed to their vehicles, which they drove recklessly toward the tracks. As drunk as they all were, they miraculously arrived all in one piece.

"I don't see any floating lights," said Gary as they all got out of their cars.

"Patience, buddy," said Bruce. "It's a virtue, y'know."

"Do we have to do anything?" asked Molly.

"They say he's more likely to come out if you stand in the middle of the tracks, but we'll have to wait half an hour before we try."

"How come?" asked Gary.

"Because Hookerman only comes out around the same time he got killed."

"How do you know so much about this stuff?" asked Molly's friend, Deena.

"My dad works for the railroad," Bruce answered.

"What'll we do 'til then?" asked Gary.

Bruce opened his car door and reached inside his glove compartment. He pulled out a small plastic bag filled with a dry, leafy material. "I bet we can think of something," he told them, grinning ear to ear.

*   *   *

After smoking what had been in his glove compartment, Bruce and his friends had gone past the point of wasted to a whole new level of personal intoxication. Even if the story Bruce was telling was completely bogus, there was still an excellent chance that they were going to see something strange happen that night—even if it was only in their imaginations.

All together, they stood along the railroad track with Bruce in front and everyone else standing behind him. There they sang songs and waited for the Hookerman to show up. Even Gary was forced to admit that he did indeed see a light floating above the railroad track.

"Bruce! Bruce!" he laughed excitedly. "You were right. I can see the Hookerman. He's floating right above me."

A chorus of voices agreed with Gary; everyone saw the light of the Hookerman.

Bruce cracked up.

"What's so funny?" asked Molly.

"You guys are so gullible," he howled.

To prove his point, he turned to face everyone and showed them all the flashlight he was holding in his right hand. "You guys will believe anything I tell you. There's no such thing as the Hookerman. It's just a stupid story my dad use to tell me whenever we went camping. It isn't—"

"Uh, Bruce," Gary interrupted him.

"What, Gary?" asked Bruce sarcastically. "Is the Hookerman really behind me? Can you see his floating lamp? Is he looking for his arm? Should I be frightened out of my mind?"

Gary decided to answer all of Bruce's questions individually. "Yeah, yeah, yeah and yeah," was his reply.

"That's BS!" said Bruce.

"Excuse me," a voice asked politely behind him, "you wouldn't happen to have seen an arm around these tracks, have you?"

Slowly Bruce turned around and saw a tall, skinny fellow who was holding up a glowing lamp with his one remaining arm. The ghost smiled at him and waited for Bruce's answer.

"Every man for himself!" was Bruce's heroic battle cry as he started running as fast as his feet could carry him. His friends immediately followed his lead and also ran screaming from the tracks.

"Kids," the old ghost said as he watched them run away. "Now, where did I leave that arm?"

Buckeye

Jordan, Doug and Stephanie were all tired when they finally stepped out of Jordan's dusty minivan. The trip to Lambertville had been a long one—close to seven hours—but it was one they had felt obligated to make. As far as they were concerned, a person couldn't be a ghost hunter without making the pilgrimage to the burned-out husk of a building that had once been Lambertville High School. For decades its reputation as a site overcrowded with spirits was known throughout the paranormal community, and though the three of them expected to capture several orbs on film before they left, that wasn't their main reason for traveling all this way.

They wanted to find out the truth about one particular spirit: Buckeye.

"Is that it?" asked Doug as they stood in front of the infamous building. "It doesn't look very imposing."

"It was a high school, Doug," Stephanie said, rolling her eyes. "Even in 1855, they tended not to make them look very Gothic."

"Yeah, I guess," Doug mumbled, obviously disappointed that he had spent seven hours driving to what looked like a fairly normal red brick building.

Jordan laughed. "Don't worry. From what I've seen it looks a lot worse on the inside."

"It better," said Doug, who was still fairly new to these ghost-hunting adventures.

"So what are we waiting for?" asked Stephanie. "Let's grab our gear and get our butts in there."

Called to action, the two men grabbed their bags out of the back of the van and followed her toward the supposedly haunted school. Stephanie attempted to open the front door. It would not budge.

"I guess we're climbing through windows again," she said with an annoyed sigh.

"Damn it," said Jordan. "We had to do that last time, and I tore a hole in my pants. They were almost brand new."

Stephanie looked at her frugal husband. "Jordan, just because you owned them for less than five years doesn't make them brand new."

"Says you," he replied.

"Will you two stop bickering and start looking for a place where we can get in here? It can't be too hard, considering how many other people have been here before us."

"How about before we go window shopping, we check out the back entrance," Jordan suggested.

Stephanie continued to tease. "Honey, you've had those pants since before we were married."

"And I like them," he answered, "so let's make sure we explore all of our doorway options before we start doing anything that might cause ripping or tearing."

Jordan started walking around the building, navigating through a large growth of weeds, uncut grass and various other forms of wild flora. Doug and Stephanie followed him and were startled when he stopped suddenly and swore with tremendous ferocity.

"Jordan, what's wrong?" Stephanie waded through the waist-high brush to get to him.

"I just tore my pants on a branch," he answered.

Stephanie and Doug both stopped in their tracks and started laughing.

"Yeah, it's hilarious," Jordan said sarcastically.

"Honey, it really is," Stephanie said as she wiped away her tears.

"Okay," he told them, "you've had your fun. Let's go."

The three of them continued to the back of the school, where they found an entrance that turned out to be much more hospitable.

"Okay, this place *is* spooky," Doug said as they walked inside and discovered what a fire and eight decades of vandalism had wrought upon the old high school's interior.

Jordan and Stephanie chorused at the same time. "Told you."

Despite all of the light coming in from outside, it was still very dark within the building, so the three of them reached into their bags and pulled out their flashlights.

"So, what happened to this place again?" asked Doug.

Stephanie pulled out her notebook, where she had jotted down the school's history after doing some research on the Internet.

"Okay, this place was first built in 1855. Then nothing interesting happened to it for 71 years. That all changed when a fire in 1926 gutted the building—"

"Did anyone die?" asked Doug.

"No," she answered, "but after they rebuilt the school's interior, almost everyone who had anything to do with the place felt that something had happened that had drastically affected its atmosphere."

"How so?" asked Jordan.

"They said the place felt colder, more imposing—like it was possessed by some kind of malevolent spirit."

"But I thought you said no one died in the fire," said Doug.

"That's the thing," answered Stephanie. "It wasn't so much that the place became haunted by a spirit anyone

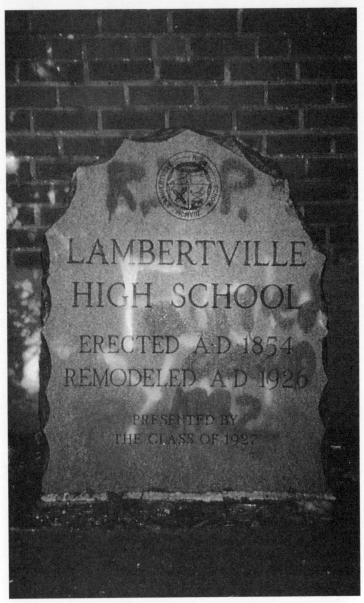

LAMBERTVILLE
HIGH SCHOOL
ERECTED A.D. 1854
REMODELED A.D. 1926

PRESENTED BY
THE CLASS OF 1927

*For decades its reputation as a site overcrowded with spirits was
known throughout the paranormal community.*

could name, but rather that the violence of the fire had done something that had permanently affected the school's ambiance."

Doug frowned. "Are you saying we drove seven hours to get to a place just because it has bad vibes?"

"No, we came here for Buckeye," said Stephanie

Doug shined his flashlight up a blackened stairway. "Okay, you're going to have to tell me this story again, because I'm not sure that I get it."

*   *   *

There's a specific kind of memory that men keep on hand so they can enjoy it during those idle moments when time allows them the luxury of a fond recollection. It is not the memory of a milestone or a significant life experience or even anything at all profound. It does not remind him of a past epiphany or an important life's lesson. It is instead the simple reminiscence of a pretty girl and how good she made him feel that first time he saw her.

Nearly every boy who attended Lambertville High School remembered the Monday morning that first brought Maria Di Novi into their lives. There had always been pretty girls at the school, but none of them had been like Maria. She was just one of those lucky people who seemed to have been born sprinkled with a touch of magical fairy dust and who went through life glowing with a sparkle not meant for us lesser mortals. Maria seemed completely oblivious to this fact, which only served to make her that much more appealing.

"Who is that?" asked Norman Fancher to his best friend, Billy Scrimshaw, when they saw her walk past them in the school's hallway.

"I don't know," Billy replied, "but I'd sure like to."

"I saw her first, Buckeye," Norman said.

"I told you not to call me that."

Norman laughed. "You're just mad because I'm calling dibs on the pretty girl."

"First off," Billy corrected him, "you can't call 'dibs' on a human being—even a really pretty one—and second off I don't like being called Buckeye because I don't like nicknames that don't make sense. What does the word even mean?"

Norman shrugged. "I don't know, but it suits you just the same."

"Well, a punch to the nose suits you just about now. You're just lucky I don't want Coach Fauss on my back for beating up the backup quarterback."

"Sure, rub it in, Buckeye," answered Norman. "Coach may have chosen you to be the starter instead of me, but that doesn't mean that little filly is going to be dumb enough to make the same mistake."

"Don't bet on it," Billy said confidently.

Norman smiled at him. "Don't worry, I won't."

*   *   *

"Are there any ghost stories that don't involve hot chicks?" Doug asked Stephanie.

"None of the good ones," answered Jordan. "Aw, dammit!"

"What's wrong?" asked Stephanie.

"I just bumped into something and got black gunk all over my pants, and it doesn't look like the kind of stuff that'll wash out."

Stephanie rolled her eyes. "Stop worrying about your stupid pants and just start taking some pictures. I bet we can get some awesome orb shots in a place like this. We came all this way, so we should get something we can put up on our web site."

"So," said Doug, "back to Buckeye. How did he get that nickname anyway?"

Stephanie shrugged. "I don't know. I couldn't find any version of the story that explained that part. I did look up the name in a dictionary, though."

"What does it mean?"

"A bunch of different things. There's a buckeye shrub and a buckeye butterfly. There's a buckeye railroad coupling and, of course, people from Ohio are called buckeyes."

"Why?"

"I don't know. I didn't think it was important enough to find out."

"Was this Billy guy originally from Ohio?"

"I don't think so. I'm pretty sure he was born and raised in New Jersey."

Doug shook his head. "If there's one thing I hate, it's nicknames that don't make sense. So who did this Maria girl end up dating?"

"Both of them," answered Stephanie.

"Ah," said Doug. "I bet that didn't go well."

*   *   *

Norman, true to his nature, made the first move. Within a week he and Maria were dating, and it was apparent from the constant grin on his face that the time he spent with her was even better than he had first imagined.

At first Billy kept his distance, partly because he didn't want to do anything to jeopardize his friendship with Norman, but also because he had found out that Maria was Catholic, and he knew that his strict Baptist parents would not approve of her. But his attraction to the girl was so strong that it became harder for him to fight it. He had tried to keep away from her for four months when Norman told him a secret as they walked home after a game.

"I'm going to ask her to marry me," he said with a satisfied smile.

"Are you serious?" asked Billy.

Norman nodded. "As a heart attack."

"When?"

"When we graduate."

"Do you think she'll say yes?"

"Of course she will, Buckeye. Why wouldn't she?"

"I don't know," Billy said, "and don't call me Buckeye."

"I already have a ring and everything."

"That's great."

"I know. I'm so excited! This girl is the prettiest thing in the whole wide world, and she's going to be my wife!"

These words lingered in Billy's brain as he got home and went into his bedroom. He thought about the idea of Maria and Norman becoming husband and wife and the more he thought about it, the less he liked it. He couldn't rid himself of the notion that Norman didn't deserve someone as special as Maria. He found himself torn between wanting to be

loyal to his best friend and wanting to be with the girl he
saw whenever he closed his eyes.

He had to act now, before Norman proposed. He had
to show Maria that she had more than one option—that
there was another quarterback for her to love.

*   *   *

"I hate ghost stories that make you wait forever to get
to the ghost part," said Doug.

"It probably doesn't help that you have the attention
span of a fruit fly," muttered Jordan under his breath.

"What was that?" asked Doug.

"Nothing," said Jordan as his camera flashed another
bright burst of light.

"Were you able to find any pictures of these folks?"
asked Doug.

"Nope," said Stephanie. "But from one of the descriptions I found, Maria probably looked a little bit like Alyssa
Milano—without the implants."

"I'm not sure I want to imagine that," said Doug.
"There are certain things in this world that are still sacred,
after all. What about Billy and Norman?"

"Typical jock types. Just imagine every guy who picked
on you in gym class."

"Gotcha," said Doug. "So basically this is a story about
two football jerks in love with the same super-hot girl?"

"Pretty much," added Stephanie.

"So why am I caring?"

"Well, someone does die and becomes an avenging
force of evil," she answered.

"Cool," said Doug. "You can carry on."

*   *   *

If Maria was as serious about Norman as Norman was about her, it definitely didn't show when Billy approached her and subtly suggested he was interested in spending some time with her. She seemed to really like the idea and even went so far as to suggest a time later that day when they could meet.

"Uh, great," said Billy, who hadn't expected all of this to happen so fast. "Where do you want to get together?"

"How about my house?"

"Won't your parents have a problem with you bringing a boy into the house?" he asked her.

"It's just me and my father," Sally said, "and he's away on business." She laughed when she noticed his face was slowly turning red. "Billy, are you blushing?"

Head quarterback or not, Billy hadn't had much experience with girls, and the thought of being alone with one—especially one as pretty as Maria—was more than enough to get his blood flowing. "I've got to get to practice," he told her, afraid he was about to embarrass himself further. "I'll see you later."

"Yes you will," she answered him with confidence.

*   *   *

"Whoa!" exclaimed Doug. "Maria's a skank!"

"Watch your language, Doug," said Jordan. "That kind of language has no place during a ghost hunt."

"Oh, stop being such a fuddy-duddy," his wife teased him. "Doug is right. Maria was clearly a skank. She was obviously dating Norman at the time, but she thought nothing of asking Billy to come to her house when she was going to be there alone. And remember this was back 80 years ago, when just holding hands with a boy could get you branded as a harlot."

"Heh, harlot," chortled Doug. "That's a funny word."

"You two really are children, aren't you?" said Jordan as he took another photograph.

*   *   *

Billy was trying hard not to shake when he knocked on Maria's front door. He had never been more nervous than he was at that moment.

"Come in," he heard her say from within the house.

With trepidation, he opened the door and walked inside. The house was small but cozy, and a wonderfully exotic smell wafted down the hallway from the kitchen.

"I'm in here," came her voice from the kitchen.

He took off his jacket and entered the kitchen, where he found Maria standing in front of a stove cooking.

"I hope you like spaghetti."

"I've never had it before," Billy said.

"You're joking, right?"

He shook his head. "My parents think eating foreign food is un-American."

"Wow. That's really…crazy."

Billy shrugged. "You can't choose your parents."

"I guess you can't," she agreed with a smile. "Now sit down and pour yourself a glass of wine. You're in for a treat; there's nothing in this world that's better than a big bowl of pasta—especially when I make it."

"Wine?"

"Of course! You have to have wine with spaghetti. Don't tell me your parents think wine is un-American, too."

"No," he said sheepishly, "just that they feel it's very immoral to drink."

"Well, try just a sip at least. I guarantee you won't go to hell."

Billy looked around—on the off chance his parents had followed him there and were spying on him from outside—before he poured himself a glass of red wine and took a little sip.

"So, what do you think?" she asked.

"I like it," Billy answered.

"Good." She smiled as she placed a bowl filled with pasta and tomato sauce in front of him. "Dig in," Maria said as she poured herself a glass of wine.

Billy picked up his fork and looked down at the meal in front of them. "Uh," he said with some embarrassment, "how do I get this all to my mouth?"

Maria laughed and showed him how to use a fork and spoon to eat the spaghetti. Following her lead, he rolled himself a large forkful and slipped it into his mouth. The taste of the sauce was filled with flavors he had never experienced before. They were warm and savory and complemented the sweetness of the tomatoes perfectly.

The pasta itself was delicious, and he couldn't wait to finish chewing it so he could have another forkful.

"This is amazing!" he said as he ate.

"I'm glad you like it." Maria smiled happily.

"I don't *like* it," he insisted. "I *love* it!"

The two of them didn't say much until they finished eating, which took some time because Billy had insisted on having a second and third helping. Finally even he was too full to have another bite, and the two of them sat in the kitchen and talked about their lives. He learned that she was originally from New York City, and she heard all about how—with Billy and Norman as quarterbacks— Lambertville High was a surefire lock to win the county championship.

Maria leaned in and whispered, "Can I tell you a secret?"

"Sure, I guess," Billy said.

"I think Norman is planning on proposing to me."

"Really? What makes you think that?"

"Women's intuition."

"What would you say if he did?"

"I don't know," Maria said. "I mean, I like him, but I don't know if I'd ever be able to love him, and I think a girl should love the man she's marrying, or else what's the point—you know what I mean?"

"I think so."

"Plus there's another fellow I've had my eye on for a while."

"Really? Who is that?"

This question made Maria laugh.

"What's so funny?" Billy asked.

"You're really not that bright are you, Billy? You don't think I make spaghetti for every boy who asks to spend some time with me, do you?"

"I did wonder," he said with a shy smile on his face.

"You're so cute, but you always seemed to keep your distance until today. How come?"

"It's stupid," he said.

"I'll bet it is. Tell me anyway."

"Norman had dibs. He saw you first."

"Oh, you boys," she sighed. "You really know how to make a girl feel special."

"I'm serious. I shouldn't be here. It's against the code."

"The code?"

"You're my best friend's girl," he told her.

Maria reached across the table and grabbed his hand. "Billy, I'm no one's girl but my own."

*   *   *

"I take it back," said Doug. "She's not a skank. She's actually pretty cool."

"She was definitely pretty liberated for a girl of that era," Jordan said as he took another photograph. "Hey, I think I got one that time."

"An orb?" asked Doug. "I thought you couldn't see those until you got the pictures developed?"

"I have a sixth sense about these things," said Jordan. "I can always tell when I've got one of those little suckers on film."

"It's strange," said his wife, "how that sixth sense of yours always kicks in when you spot a fluff ball floating in the air."

"So what happened next with Billy and Maria? Did they do it?" asked Doug.

"Of course not," answered Stephanie. "Billy was a gentlemen. Plus his parents would have killed him if they found out he had premarital sex—literally."

"But they did still keep seeing each other behind Norman's back, right?"

"Oh, of course."

*   *   *

For a whole month, Billy and Maria were able to keep their clandestine relationship a secret, but it was only a matter of time before they were found out. One of Billy's other teammates saw the two of them walking together hand in hand in a park and told Norman about it the next day.

Norman grew so enraged by the news that when he found Billy he grabbed him by his shirt and slammed him against the side of the school.

"Are you trying to steal my girl?" he shouted at his friend.

Billy was so shocked by this accusation that he said the first thing that came to his mouth. "I can't steal something that doesn't belong to you!"

Stunned by these words, Norman let go of his friend and took a step back. "What did you just say?"

"She's her own girl, Norman," Billy explained. "Neither of us owns her. It's up to her to decide who she wants to be with."

Norman responded to this by making a loud reference to male bovine excrement.

"Good," said Billy, "keep thinking that way. Then I'm sure she'll wind up choosing me."

"Like hell," said Norman. "There's no way I'm going to let that happen."

"How are you going to stop her?"

Norman did not have an answer for this question, so he screamed out with frustration instead. A minute passed as the two of them stood there glaring at each other.

Norman finally broke the silence. "We have to settle this," he said.

"How?"

"Doing what we do best," he answered.

Billy immediately understood what he was talking about. "When?"

"Tomorrow after practice. We'll tell the team to stick around, and we'll divide them into two equal teams and the person with the highest score at the end gets to keep seeing Maria, while the loser agrees to never talk to her again."

"Sounds good to me," said Billy.

"Good," sneered Norman.

He turned away, leaving Billy to mourn the death of their friendship and to consider the possibility that after tomorrow he might never be able to talk to the girl he loved ever again.

*   *   *

"Okay," said Doug, "just so we're clear—they're going to play a football game, right?"

"What else would they be talking about? Cricket?" asked Jordan.

"I don't know, I just wanted to be sure. So are we getting any closer to the ghost part?"

"We're almost there," answered Stephanie.

"About freaking time," Doug said. "I was beginning to think it was never going to happen."

*   *   *

Maria didn't take kindly to the news that she was to be the prize in a football contest.

"Shouldn't I have a choice in the matter?" she asked Billy when he told her what had happened.

"I told you," he said, "this is about the code. You don't have to stay with the winner if you don't want to, but Norman and I have to do this. It's just the way it is."

"Why are boys so stupid?" she asked.

"I don't know. We just are."

"What if I make my decision right now? What if I choose today? Would the two of you still have to play that stupid game?"

"Yes," he answered, "we would."

"Fine," she said in disgust. "Just don't expect me to be there to watch it happen."

"We won't."

Word quickly spread among Lambertville High's student body about Billy and Norman's big game after school. By the time the fateful hour arrived, every student—except one—was there surrounding the football field, waiting for the game to begin. But first the two former best friends had to pick their teams. They flipped a coin to see who would be the first to choose among their fellow teammates. Billy won. With this advantage, he decided to build a fast, offensive team, hoping that his skills as a quarterback would make up for a weaker defense. Norman went the opposite route and picked all of Lambertville's biggest players, hoping that their size would allow them to dominate the smaller team.

The officials for the game were chosen from the players that neither Norman nor Billy had selected, and with them the two boys laid out the rules. There weren't many. The game was to last one hour. The captain whose team had the most points by the end of that hour won the right to be Maria's boyfriend, and the loser had to vow to never talk to her again. They tossed the coin one more time to determine starting advantage, and Billy won once again. He decided to receive.

As different as the two teams were in terms of size and style, it soon became clear that they were very evenly matched. After 50 minutes of play they were tied 14–14. With 10 minutes left to gain the advantage before the game went into sudden death overtime, Billy called time out and gathered his team together into a huddle.

"Okay guys," he told his team, "what I need you to do is ignore Klayman, but in a way that doesn't seem deliberate."

Klayman was Dennis Klayman, a large, homely boy who was universally regarded as the dimmest bulb to ever attend Lambertville High. His size had earned him a spot on both the school and Norman's team, but his skills were such that he had never actually touched the ball in the past three years.

"What's the thinking here, Billy?" asked one of his players.

"If we can get Norman to believe that we're not even going to bother attempting to guard Klayman, then there's a chance he might actually throw a pass to him—"

"Which we'll be able to intercept without a problem," a voice said as they all clued into their captain's logic.

When the sound of the referee's whistle signaled the end of the time out, they set their plan into action. Norman's team had the ball and was moving slowly down the field. Over the course of five minutes they made it to the 40-yard line, while Billy's team left Klayman open and alone during every play.

Norman noticed his teammate's lack of opposition on the field, but he failed to realize it was a deliberate trap. Just like Billy had hoped he would, he assumed that they were leaving Klayman alone because of their disdain for his offensive abilities. Playing directly into his former best friend's plans, he decided to take a chance and throw a pass to the oaf, if only because—he thought—such a move would be totally unexpected.

The play began, and Norman pretended he was going to pass to another, well-guarded teammate, when he suddenly turned and threw the ball as hard as he could to Klayman. From out of nowhere Billy appeared beside the seemingly open player and Norman screamed out an obscenity and closed his eyes when he realized he had been set up. His curse was still echoing in the air when the cheering crowd fell suddenly—eerily—silent.

Norman opened his eyes and saw his best friend lying in a crumpled heap on the field. In that instant he completely forgot why they had been playing the game and ran to Billy.

"What happened?" he asked Klayman with a panicked roar.

"The ball," Klayman tried to explain. "Billy ran toward it so fast, but he didn't catch it. It hit him in the face, and he fell down."

"Billy!" Norman shouted as he bent over his fallen friend. "Billy, are you all right? Billy—say something!"

Billy stayed silent and did not stir.

He was dead.

*   *   *

"About freaking time," cheered Doug. "I was beginning to think this was the first ghost story where no one died."

"Patience is a virtue, young one," said Jordan as he snapped another photograph.

"There's just one thing I don't get," Doug admitted.

"What's that?" asked Stephanie.

"The part where he dies. How'd that happen?"

"It was a freak accident," Stephanie explained. "Norman had thrown the ball with so much power that when it hit Billy in the face it snapped his head back so hard that he broke his neck and died instantly."

Doug winced. "Ouch, that'll do it. So I guess this is followed by the part where Norman is stricken with guilt and vows to never talk to Maria again?"

"Hey!" said Stephanie. "Who's telling this story anyway?"

*   *   *

There is a strong paranormal presence near the staircase.

Norman was stricken with guilt and—after the funeral of his friend—vowed to never talk to Maria again. She did not mind, especially because, had she been given a choice like she had wanted, she would have chosen Billy.

Following the tragic game, Norman quit the football team and became something of a loner. He stopped spending time with his friends and wandered the school's hallways like a sad, pale ghost.

He spent a lot of his time sitting at the stairwell where he and Billy used to eat their lunch when it was cold outside. That was the last place where anyone saw him alive.

Afternoon classes had just started when a blood-curdling scream echoed throughout the hallway. Teachers and students rushed out of their classes to catch sight of the cause of this commotion.

What they found was Norman's body crumpled in a heap at the base of the school's staircase.

His neck was broken.

*   *   *

"Cool," said Doug. "That means he was found dead right where I'm standing!"

"Give or take a couple of inches," confirmed Stephanie.

*   *   *

At first everyone assumed that Norman had fallen from the top of the stairs, but when his body was examined it was found to be completely free of any of the kind of bruising that would have inevitably resulted during this kind of accident. Apart from his broken neck, there was no sign of any other kind of physical trauma. Some suggested he had committed suicide, but they were unable to explain how he might have pulled it off.

It was only a matter of days before the students at the school began to speculate that his death was not an accident or suicide, but murder. At first some people suspected that he had been killed by Maria as revenge for killing the boy she loved, but anyone who had ever seen the tiny beauty standing next to Norman knew that there was no way she was physically capable of breaking his neck.

But, as impossible as it was to believe that Maria was the murderer, the other possibility that was suggested was even more difficult to accept—could Norman have been killed by Billy's angry ghost?

The fact that they both died with the same injury was believed by many to be a clue that Billy's spirit had returned from the grave and made sure that his death was avenged. Some people even went so far as to suggest that Billy's spirit had done the deed with a phantom football he had hurled at Norman's head with terminal force.

From all this speculation an urban legend began to grow. According to this legend, a person could find out for certain how Norman Fancher had died simply by standing where he was found dead and shouting out the following phrase: "Hey, Buckeye—do you want a game?" The answer was short and quick: an impossibly fast sphere of ghostly light would hit the questioner so hard in the head that it would kill him or her instantly.

How many people managed to test the veracity of this legend and lived to tell about it is unknown.

*   *   *

"Oh come on!" said Doug. "You actually expect me to believe that if I stand here and say that, I'll be killed?"

"That's the legend of Buckeye," shrugged Stephanie. "How are you doing, honey?" she asked Jordan.

"I think I'm good," Jordan answered. "I've shot enough rolls that there's no way I haven't gotten something on film. We can probably head on out if you want."

"I'm just thinking that if we leave now we won't be too tired for work tomorrow."

"Okay," smiled Doug, "I know what's supposed to happen now. You guys walk out of here and leave me alone in this place and I—like a jerk—say what I'm not supposed to say and you guys hear this scream come from inside the school, so you run back in and find me dead on the ground with a broken neck. Right?"

"It doesn't *have* to happen that way," said Stephanie.

"It's totally up to you," added Jordan.

With that, the two of them turned away from Doug and walked out of the old, abandoned schoolhouse. Doug stood there at the base of the blackened staircase and looked up into the darkness into which its steps led. He knew that there was only one way to find out if the story of Buckeye was true or not.

*   *   *

Stephanie and Jordan were busy packing their bags back into the minivan when they heard a horrible scream come from inside the schoolhouse. Their eyes widened and their hearts stopped.

"Doug!" they both shouted as they ran back to the school.

They were both breathless by the time they made it back inside and found Doug on the floor—laughing so hard tears were coming out of his eyes.

He howled with delight as they stood there and glared at him. "You guys thought I was dead."

"I take it you've just proven that the story isn't true," said Stephanie with a look of disapproval.

"Are you nuts?" asked Doug. "I'm not suicidal. I didn't say anything to provoke any spirit that may or may not haunt this building. I just screamed because I thought it would be funny if you thought I had died—and I was right. It was *hilarious.*"

"You're a true comedian," growled Jordan. "Now let's get out of here."

"Okay, grouchy," Doug said, still smiling as he stood up and started following them as they made their way back to the van. "Wouldn't it be cool," he suggested, "if something happened right now that caused an accident that broke my neck and killed me? Wouldn't that be super ironic?"

Stephanie and Jordan just turned and glared at him.

"I mean," he continued, "isn't that how a good ghost story is supposed to end?"

The
Dutchman

There are some people in this world who seem as though they were born to be other people's sport. Sad, hapless folks upon whom destiny has laden a combination of personality and appearance that dooms them to forever be the targets of other people's mockery, they live each day hearing the laughter of others, knowing that it comes at their expense. Such is the cruelty of fate that very few of these poor souls ever find the strength required to break out of their roles of unwitting jesters and, despite being the cause of so much amusement, die having led unhappy lives. And in the worst cases—the ones where fate's humor is at its very blackest—even death is not enough to make the laughing stop.

Rambout Van Dam was a small, round man cursed with a mop of unruly blond hair, buckteeth and two large ears that stuck straight out from the side of his head. He was the youngest son in a family of cobblers who plied their trade all across the Netherlands, but unlike the rest of his family, he was not blessed with the talents required of a competent shoemaker. The shoes he crafted were not just uncomfortable; they actually caused anyone who tried them on to scream in agony as they attempted to walk in them for just a few short steps. The pain was so intense that—had it occurred to anyone—the shoes could have successfully been sold as instruments of torture to all of the castles around Europe that still maintained fully functioning dungeons.

His father feared that the longer Rambout plied the family trade at home, the more damage he would do to their reputation for quality craftsmanship. He knew he had to get his son out of the country so that Rambout's horrible shoes would no longer sully the Van Dam name. Opportunity struck when an acquaintance told him about a group of people who had booked a ship for the purpose of traveling to the newly discovered continent, where they planned on settling in the Dutch colony known as New Amsterdam. Rambout's father went to the man in charge of the group and asked him if the colony needed any cobblers. It turned out that it did, and Rambout, before he even had any idea of what was going on, found himself on a boat sailing across the ocean to the New World.

The ship's other passengers made no effort at all to befriend the young cobbler, so the long journey proved to be a lonely one for Rambout. The only time anyone acknowledged him was when he fell down, which was something he tended to do quite a lot—especially when the waters were choppy. On those occasions they would point and laugh at him, even when it was apparent that he had actually hurt himself.

He was hobbling around on a twisted ankle when the large boat finally reached its destination. Upon arriving in the colony, his fellow passengers decided they no longer needed a cobbler, and they abandoned him to his own devices. With the little bit of money his father had given him he ended up in the town of Bergin, where he opened up a small cobbler's shop and made a pittance by repairing shoes, albeit very badly (the townspeople having quickly learned to never wear any of the shoes he made).

Although he tried his best to fit into his new community, no one made any attempt to make him feel at home. They were too busy laughing at him, amused by his large front teeth, messy hair and great big ears. They howled at his clumsiness and mocked his attempts to make friends and be sociable.

"I almost feel sorry for the oaf," one townsperson said to another as they wiped tears from their eyes following a hilarious incident in which Rambout had managed to fall into a nearby horse trough.

"I know," said the other. "If I were that ridiculous, I would drown myself rather than have everyone laughing at me."

This statement was the common consensus throughout the community. Everyone wondered how Rambout could go on living, knowing that he was such a fool. The obvious answer was that somehow the incompetent cobbler didn't know that he was an idiot. And his cluelessness only made it that much easier to laugh at him.

Eventually, people started to get tired of simply waiting for him to do something stupid, so they started playing practical jokes on him whenever they wanted some cheap amusement. From Monday through Saturday, they all took turns setting up situations that were intended to make him look even more foolish than usual. The only reason they left him alone on Sunday was that the principles of the Dutch Reformed Church forbid doing much of anything on the Sabbath, except going to church and resting, like the Lord intended.

But it didn't take long for these malicious jokers to notice that Rambout was obviously lonely. This realization did little to make them any more sympathetic toward him. If anything, it merely gave them a new vein of cruelty to mine.

"Have you heard about the dances that they throw at Tappen Zee?" one of these jokers said loudly to his friend when they noticed Rambout walking by.

His friend played along. "No, tell me more."

"Well, there they play the best music and you can dance with all of these pretty girls who are looking to find a good husband." He went on before pretending to notice the clumsy cobbler. "Oh, hello, Rambout. How are you doing today?"

"I'm good," Rambout answered him. "I couldn't help but overhear you say something about a party."

"That's right," the joker said and smiled. "Over at Tappen Zee. They hold it every Saturday night. It's the perfect place for a bachelor like yourself to find a nice girl. You should think about going."

"Maybe I will," said Rambout. "Thank you for telling me about it."

"You're welcome," said the joker, who was literally pinching himself to keep from laughing out loud.

"Is there really a party at Tappen Zee?" asked his friend when Rambout was gone.

The joker laughed. "Who knows? Anything's possible. Although, if there is, I highly doubt there would be any women there desperate enough to dance with someone like him."

As Rambout went about his day, he thought of how fun it would be to go to a party and maybe talk and dance with a pretty girl. He even allowed himself to daydream about the possibility of being given a kiss by one of these imaginary young ladies. He had never been kissed before by anyone other than his grandmother, and he knew that

His shoes could have been successfully sold as instruments of torture.

she didn't count. He decided that on Saturday he would row his leaky little boat over to Tappen Zee and see if he couldn't make his happy little daydream come true.

When the day came, Rambout put on his finest clothes and stepped into his rowboat and started rowing across the Hudson River toward Tappen Zee. The water was rough, and it took him quite a bit longer than he had thought it would, but eventually he got there. He realized when he made it to shore that he wasn't sure where the party was, so he asked the first person he came across.

What the joker who had told him about the party didn't know was that a dance had actually been organized to take place at Tappen Zee that Saturday. The young man Rambout had come across was on his way there. Rambout followed him and was indeed amazed by how many pretty girls were in attendance.

Had this been a party held in Bergin, those pretty girls would have ignored the little cobbler, except maybe to laugh at him when he asked them to dance, but the people who lived in Tappen Zee were of a much kinder and more generous temperament. Although he was not their ideal choice for a dance partner, the young ladies he asked to dance with were only too happy to oblige him with a quick trip around the room. They soon found that the clumsy cobbler was actually a very good dancer; his normal lack of coordination turned into graceful movement when set to music. His skill on the dance floor made him popular, and by the end of the night he had danced with every single girl who had been there. Even though he did not get his kiss, he did get asked to come to next Saturday's dance.

It had been the best night of his life, and he had had so much fun that he had completely lost track of the time. It was 11 o'clock, and he had only one hour to get home without breaking the Sabbath. Although he was not very religious himself, his neighbors were, and if they caught him coming home after midnight, he could get into serious trouble.

Unfortunately, the river was even rougher than it had been earlier that evening. No matter how hard he rowed, he couldn't get any forward momentum. The waves started rising and splashing around him, and storm clouds rose ominously over his head, showering him with rain and frightening him with equal measures of thunder and lightning.

The poor little cobbler did not make it home.

Neither he nor his rowboat was ever found. No one in Bergin mourned his disappearance, and many townspeople even felt he had gotten what he deserved for traveling on the Sabbath. Soon the townspeople found a new fool to make fun of and started erasing Rambout Van Dam from their minds.

But he would not be so easily forgotten.

Within months of his passing, people started seeing a phantom rowboat traveling across the river. The figure at its oars was unmistakable. Despite all of the cruelty he had suffered while living in Bergin, his spirit was still determined to find its way home, but no matter how hard the Dutchman rowed, he has never been able to reach his destination.

Eventually, Bergin became Jersey City, New Jersey, but the little cobbler's determination remained undiminished. To this day his spirit can be spotted rowing across the Hudson River. Hopefully someday soon he'll finally find his way home.

The Gentleman Thief

It would have been a very quiet night in the small, now-forgotten town of Washington, New Jersey, were it not for the sound of young woman crying in the backyard of the local tavern. She was trying hard to fight against her tears, but her situation was so dire that she could not hope to hold them back, and she visibly shook from the force of them. No one paid her any attention. Everyone inside the tavern knew why she was crying, but no one made any attempt to comfort her. It wasn't apathy that kept them away—they simply could not think of anything to do or say that would change her situation or ease her sorrow.

It would take a stranger to accept that challenge.

As she cried, she felt a large hand take hold of her left shoulder. She turned to see a tall, handsome man dressed in a long coat standing before her. She had never seen him before and had no idea who he could be.

"If there is one thing in this world more ugly than the sight of a pretty girl's tears, I cannot imagine what it could be," he told her in a strong, clear voice that could only belong to someone who possessed the confidence and power of a Titan.

"I'm sorry, sir," she said, "but I cannot think of anything else to do. In one hour I shall be dead."

"Dead?"

"Yes, sir. Dead."

"And how could you possibly know this?"

"Because that is when I shall be forced to take my own life," she said.

"What?" he exclaimed, scandalized by her words. "Who would dare compel you to suicide?"

"Simon Atherton," she answered. "The banker."

"I don't understand," said the man. "Tell me your story, pretty girl, so I can rid myself of this vexing confusion."

The girl's name was Gloria—Gloria Calleia—and she was the daughter of a local farmer. Times had been tough for their family. Gloria's mother had died giving birth to her little brother, who himself lived only a week after that, leaving Gloria and her father all alone. He could barely manage the farm by himself and could not afford to hire anyone to help him. Their crops began to fail. Their livestock took ill and died. All of their money dried up, and they could not afford to pay the mortgage on the land. Simon Atherton, who held the mortgage, was ready to foreclose on the property and take everything the Calleias owned to settle their debt. But when his eyes first caught sight of the farmer's beautiful daughter, he came up with another solution instead.

"He told me that if I wanted my father to keep our farm, I would have to become his wife," Gloria explained to the stranger.

"There are worse fates than being a rich man's wife," said the man.

"Not if the way that man made his fortune was by being heartless and cruel," she told him. "I would consider him vile if he did what he did and took no pleasure in it, but I have seen the thrill he gets each time he hurts someone. It is not that he has no heart, but that his heart is fueled by hate. The thought of being married to someone so sadistic is one I cannot bear the burden of. The ceremony is to take place in this tavern in one hour, and when it is over and Atherton hands over the deed to our farm to my father, I shall cut my own throat."

"You will do no such thing," the man stated.

"But there is no other option! It is the difference between a long, slow death that lasts a lifetime or one that is quick and painless. What kind of fool would I be if didn't choose the latter?"

"There is another option," said the man.

"No, there isn't! I've thought of every possibility! This is the only way," she said sobbing.

"Stop your crying! I am a man of my word, and I promise I shall get you out of this!"

"But how?"

"Don't concern yourself with that. Just dry your eyes and rid the world of such an ugly sight."

The man turned away from her and went into the tavern. Gloria did as she was told and wiped away her tears, then waited for what she prayed would be her salvation.

The hour passed quickly, and Atherton arrived to meet his future bride. He was a small, twisted man, old enough to be her grandfather. The grin on his face was so disgusting with its promise of undisguised carnality that it was nearly impossible to look upon it. He looked not so much like a man as a vulture licking its beak in anticipation of its next meal. With him was the local justice of the peace, who looked extremely uncomfortable in his role as the solemnizer of this union.

As the ceremony began, Gloria's gaze kept darting over to the stranger, who sat in the back of the tavern with the brim of his hat obscuring his face. She prayed that he would keep his promise, fully prepared to take the ultimate action upon herself if he did not.

The justice of the peace cleared his throat and began to speak. Gloria grew tense as each second passed and the stranger did nothing. It was only when she heard the words, "If there is anyone here who has cause to see this ceremony cease, speak now or forever hold your peace," that she realized her savior had been waiting for the right dramatic moment.

"I have cause," shouted a voice from the back.

Shocked, Atherton turned around and searched with his eyes for the source of this interruption.

"Who said that?" he hissed angrily.

"I did," said the stranger as he stood up from his seat.

"And who are you?"

"They call me Joe Mulliner."

The people in the tavern gasped when they heard the man's name.

All of the color drained from Atherton's face. "Not *the* Joe Mulliner?" he asked weakly.

"I am afraid, sir, that you will find there is but one Joe Mulliner in this part of the world, and I am he," said the stranger.

"What are you doing here?" asked Atherton. "What business do you have stopping my wedding? I have never done anything to you."

"Yes you have," said Mulliner. "Because of you I was forced to take in the dreadful sight of this beautiful woman in a state of utter sadness. It is a crime I am not compelled to forgive."

Atherton turned to Gloria. "What did you say to him?" he asked her angrily.

"I told him the truth," she answered quietly.

Atherton roared with rage and slapped her harshly across the face with the back of his hand, but before he could strike her again, he was stopped by the sight of a musket pointed at his head.

"Hit her again," said Mulliner, "and it will be the very last thing you do."

"You won't get away with this," said Atherton.

"You do realize," Mulliner answered back, "that it is never wise to threaten a man who has a weapon pointed in your direction. Now, this is what is going to happen: you are going to hand the deed to Mr. Calleia's farm over to him, and then you are going to leave and never trouble these good people again. If I find out that you have attempted to mete out even the most insignificant form of retribution upon them, I will come back here and kill you where you stand. Do you understand?"

Atherton's face was a scarlet mask of rage, but there was nothing he could do. He knew enough about the reputation of the man threatening him to stay quiet and hand over the pertinent document to Gloria's extremely puzzled father. He then turned and stormed out of the tavern. He never bothered the Calleias again.

Gloria was so relieved that she burst into tears of joy. "I'm sorry, I know how you hate to see a woman cry," she said to Mulliner.

"Nonsense," he said with a smile. "I hate to see tears of sadness. Tears of happiness, on the other hand, are a true pleasure to behold." He put away his musket and gave Gloria a long, hard hug, then let her go and turned to face the tavern's crowd. "There may not have been a wedding tonight, but I don't see why we can't have a party!"

Everyone roared with approval.

"And I'm sure Mr. Atherton will be kind enough to pay for it!" he added, causing an even louder roar to follow.

It was the loudest, most raucous party ever to be held in the small town, and all of the people who were there remembered it to the last of their days. Joe Mulliner laughed and drank and danced with every woman there, starting with Gloria. When he had finally had his fill, he took Gloria aside and was seen whispering something in her ear. She refused to tell anyone what he said to her, but that didn't stop people from speculating upon all of the possibilities.

There was something obviously extraordinary about Joe Mulliner, even from his earliest days. Born in 1746 to a wealthy New Jersey family, he was always the tallest, the strongest, the handsomest, the slyest and the loudest man wherever he went. For a time he was content to employ his gifts as an honest man, but when the Revolutionary War began, he found it easier to use them to defy the law. He became New Jersey's most famous gentleman thief. They called him "the Robin Hood of the Pine Barrens."

Well-educated and trained in all of the ways of polite society, young Joe married a woman of exquisite beauty named Anna. If there was one thing in this world that Joe loved more than any other, it was beautiful women—and they loved him right back. Although he was never faithful to her, Anna loved him too much to care. She was happy merely to have been able to have the first claim on him.

The two of them lived on a small farm near the Mullica River, but fate kept him from living there for very long. The colonies were edging closer and closer to starting a war that would see them seceding from England, and men were being forced to choose between being loyal to their king or to their new homeland. His brothers sided with the colonies and joined the Revolutionary army, but Joe insisted on staying loyal to his king and country. This decision was not an idle one; it made him extremely unpopular with his neighbors, and he risked arrest as a traitor to the acting colonial government. Had the farm he shared with Anna not been purchased in her father's name, it would have been seized. As it was, Joe was forced to flee, leaving behind both his home and his lovely wife.

Although he could have joined the British army and fought against the colonists who had forced him from his home, Joe decided that he was not someone who was meant to take part in war—even if he thought the cause was just. Again this decision was not lightly made, as it made him an outcast to both sides of the rebellion. He was truly an outsider who—despite his loyalty to the Crown—owed no allegiance to anyone but himself.

He was not alone. Not far from his home on the Mullica River he came across a group of men whose circumstances were similar to his own—they refused to rebel against England, but wanted no part in the war against the colonists. They called themselves "the Refugees," and they took their refuge on an island known as The Forks, which sat in the middle of the Mullica, just a half-mile from his old home. Some of these Refugees were honest men like Joe who had come to The Forks as an act of conscience, but others were not so honorable and had gathered there out of a twisted sense of self-interest. This latter group was largely composed of men who had spent their lives in the criminal fraternity. Surrounded by thieves, Joe decided that if he and his fellow Refugees were to survive, he would have to take control of this criminal element and lead it in directions that could help rather than hinder them.

He explained to his men that if they were to prosper, they could not act like savages; they must behave like gentlemen. "If we are to be thieves," he told them, "then we shall be thieves of good conscience. We shall commit no acts of violence without cause, and we shall only steal from those who can afford to be robbed. Let the rich hate and fear us; we shall be safe as long as the poor believe we are truly on their side."

*   *   *

Trevor Leland could not hide his anxiousness as his coach traveled along a dirt road through the New Jersey countryside.

"My darling, why do you look so pale?" asked his lovely wife, Belinda.

"The motion of the coach is unpleasant to my stomach," he lied. "It makes me feel quite ill."

The truth he did not want his wife to know was that a rash of robberies had occurred along this road, and he was afraid that they too would suffer such an attack. He kept his hand close to the pistol he had bought for the journey, even though he had never fired one before and didn't know if he had the nerve to pull the trigger if the situation demanded it.

As the hours passed and the night appeared to be close to ending, he started to relax, hoping that they were out of the danger zone. His hopes were dashed, however, when he heard the sound of shouting and the coach came to a sudden halt. Before he could react, the door to the coach burst open, and he and his wife were greeted by the warm smile of a large and handsome man.

"Greetings to you two tonight," said the man. "I hope your travels thus far haven't been too difficult. Ah!" he added when he noticed Trevor's hand move toward his pistol. "I see that you have been wise enough to take the proper precautions for this kind of journey. Good for you! I am afraid, however, that in your hands such an instrument might cause unnecessary harm, so I'm going to have to ask you to hand it over to me for safekeeping."

"I shall do no such thing!" Trevor said indignantly.

"I am going to have to insist, sir," said the stranger as he pulled out a pistol of his own and pointed it at Trevor's chest.

Trevor's survival instinct kicked in. "Here you go," he said as he handed over the weapon.

"Thank you kindly," the man said, smiling as he slipped the gun into one of his cloak's pockets. "Now I'm going to have to ask for all of your jewelry, bank notes, coins and anything else that might be of value."

"Trevor!" Belinda shouted at her husband. "How can you let this happen? Do something!"

The stranger turned his attention to the coach's more attractive passenger. "I wouldn't speak so crossly with your husband, Ma'am," he suggested to her kindly. "He's in a very trying situation, and he's attempting to get the two of you through it with a minimum of fuss."

Belinda was struck silent by the man's sincerity and found herself strangely drawn to him. For a moment she almost forgot he was stealing the jewelry that adorned her fingers, wrists and neck.

Within two minutes the stranger had taken everything the couple had of value on their persons. "It was a pleasure to do business with you this early morning," he said. "I think the only thing that could make it better is if I were to steal a kiss from your lovely wife," he told Trevor.

"Go ahead, you've taken everything else," his victim shrugged and said.

"You are so kind," the man laughed before he bestowed a long, passionate kiss upon Belinda's lips. "Now I am off," he said with a flourish when he was done. He disappeared back outside, and the astonished couple heard the sound of horses riding away.

Trevor jumped out of the coach and saw its driver cowering in his seat. "Don't just sit there," he shouted at the man. "Go after them! Or, if you're too cowardly to do that, we can at least find the nearest lawman."

The coachman shook his head. "No, sir, I cannot. They told me quite firmly that bad things would happen if I were to move in any direction for the next two hours, and I believe them."

Trevor couldn't blame the poor man for being so frightened, so he merely grumbled and returned inside the coach, where he found his wife fanning herself with her hat.

"Who was that man?" she asked her husband, her voice quaking with relief and excitement.

"I don't know," Trevor said, "but I have to admit that he's good at what he does."

"*Very* good," his wife added.

*   *   *

Within a very short time the people of the Pine Barrens could talk of little else but their region's famous gentleman thief. The comparisons to the famous nobleman bandit of Sherwood Forest came almost immediately. The area's poorest residents told of how, when they were confronted by Joe's band of refugees, they were allowed to go on untouched, with all of their belongings still in their possession. Joe became famous for stealing only from the wealthy and for doing so using the most genial and affable methods possible. Not everyone escaped from the gang uninjured, but those who were hurt during these confrontations inevitably suffered because they had made the first attack. Joe and his men used their weapons only for self-defense—they never shot first. And sometimes, on those rare occasions when his men had been forced to become physical with their victims, Joe would even go so far as to return some of money that they had stolen as a gesture of goodwill.

The most famous account of this arose when a band of his men decided to rob a widow named Freda Bates while Joe was off somewhere else. Knowing she was a church-going woman, they contrived to rob her home while she was away at that morning's Sunday service. Unfortunately, they had misjudged the time she was to be away and were only halfway done when she returned.

"What are you doing here?" she shouted angrily.

The bandits attempted to use the same techniques they had seen Joe employ to keep his victims calm, but she proved to be completely unsusceptible to this combination of good manners, charm and flattery.

"You filthy, no-good, thieving rascals!" she said, using the strongest language she was capable of before she picked up a nearby broomstick and began swatting them with it.

Trying their best not to hurt her, they grabbed her and took away her broom. She cursed at them and struggled to get out of their grasp, so they had no choice but to take her outside and tie her to a nearby tree. From there her language grew significantly saltier; her vocabulary was filled with words she had never felt the need to speak before.

As she went on a long tirade about the low morals of the bandits' mothers, they tried their best to ignore her and went about their work, finishing the job they had started. Unfortunately for Mrs. Bates, one of her insults was heard by a member of the Refugee gang who had very strong feelings about his mother and who did not take kindly to hearing her memory so recklessly slandered. His face turned bright crimson with anger as he ran out of the house and ordered the old woman to take back what she had just said.

"I will do no such thing. Your actions here serve as proof that everything I have just said is 100 percent correct."

"You take it back, old woman," the bandit said, "or there will be consequences."

Joe Mulliner visited many taverns throughout New Jersey.

"Do your worst!" replied Mrs. Bates. "I'm not afraid of you, you dirty son of a—" She continued to use words not usually acceptable in polite society.

The bandit decided to call her bluff and took a pack of matches out of his pocket. He lit one and—in front of Mrs. Bates—held its flame to a loose piece of wood connected to the porch of her house.

Mrs. Bates gasped. "What are you doing? Stop that at once!"

The bandit ignored her. Within a few seconds the piece of wood began to burn, and the flame started to move quickly across the porch.

"You all better hurry!" he shouted to his fellow Refugees, who were still inside the house. They quickly noticed the smoke and flames and ran out of the house through the back door as the whole building began to burn.

Mrs. Bates sobbed as she watched her home erupt into a blazing fire. The bandits left her tied up to the tree, justifiably fearing what she would do to them if they set her free. Not long after they left, a neighbor noticed the smoke in the air and ran to get help. Mrs. Bates was freed, and the fire was quelled before it spread, but her house was destroyed beyond repair.

A week and a half later, while she was staying with a friend, she received a package that contained $300, but no written message indicating who it was from. Both she and the rest of the community came to the same conclusion: the money came directly from Joe Mulliner and was his way of apologizing for what his men had done.

*   *   *

As his reputation grew, Joe's love of a good party grew more and more dangerous for him to indulge in. He risked arrest every time he lingered in public for longer than a few minutes. Still, he was not detered in the slightest.

At one well-known gathering in the town of Quaker Bridge (just five miles northwest of the small town where he had saved Gloria Calleia from her dreadful fate) Joe arrived and—as he always did—selected the prettiest woman in attendance as his dancing partner. Like so many of his previous dancing partners, this young lady had not come to the party alone. However, unlike almost all of the other men who found themselves forced to watch as their wives and fiancées danced with the handsome thief, her escort refused to play the wallflower. When Mulliner approached the woman and asked her to dance, the small man told the famous bandit that she was spoken for. Mulliner just laughed and pushed the small man aside. Before the man even knew what he was doing, he lifted up his hand and slapped Mulliner roughly across his face. At once the music stopped, and gasps were heard in the silence that followed. Everyone waited to see how Mulliner would react to having been struck by a man nearly half his size. People closed their eyes, not wanting to see the poor man shot dead or cut through with a knife.

But instead of killing the man, Joe surprised everyone by laughing with delight. "Such bravery in a little soul such as this deserves the finest girl in the room!" he shouted as he shook the man's hand. He then proceeded to turn once around the dance floor with the young woman before he handed her back over to the small fellow. Joe then left the party as everyone buzzed about the exciting scene they had just witnessed.

Unfortunately for the Pine Barrens' famous highwayman, he crashed one party too many when he made his usual noisy entrance at a gathering being held at the Indian Cabin Mill Inn in the town of Nesco. Just like he had in Quaker Bridge, he immediately found the prettiest girl in the room and shoved aside her escort so that he could dance with her. This time he did not get slapped; instead, the jealous young suitor left the party and found the leader of the local militia, Captain Baylin, and informed him that the leader of the Refugees was at that moment dancing up a storm just a short walk away.

As he always did, Joe selected the prettiest woman in attendance as his dancing partner.

Baylin had long ago vowed to capture the popular bandit and wasted little time raising a posse and surrounding the inn. Outnumbered and outgunned, Mulliner knew he had no hope of escaping. Fearing that engaging in any kind of fight would result in the loss of innocent lives, he did the only thing he could do and surrendered.

He was taken to the town of Burlington where he was tried for the crime of high treason. On August 8, 1781, he was found guilty and hanged that same day. His body was sent back to his wife, Anna, who buried him on the small farm he had fled back before he had become a legend. His grave was marked with a small stone that simply read "JM."

Following his death, his legend did not fade—if anything, Joe Mulliner became more famous than he had been before. In 1855, 74 years after his execution, a writer named Charles J. Peterson wrote a novel entitled *Kate*

Aylesford or, the Heiress of Sweetwater, which was based on the famous story of a young woman named Honoria Read, who was said to have once been kidnapped by Mulliner after he took exception to not having been invited to the lavish party she was hosting at her home in Pleasant Mills. Although most of the book is purely fictional, many of its details became firmly attached to Mulliner's legend.

But more than any book, two things kept the memory of the Pine Barrens' own Robin Hood alive. First, there were rumors of buried treasure. Second, there were tales that his spirit remained on this earth, either (depending on who you asked) to guard that treasure or to find it once again.

Many people have speculated over the years about just what Joe Mulliner whispered into Gloria Calleia's ear that one night their paths crossed and her life was forever changed. The reason for this speculation is that, not long after Mulliner essentially banished Simon Atherton away from the small town of Washington, Gloria and her father suddenly came into a small fortune. With it they were able to pay all of their debts (except for the one owed to Atherton, of course), and Gloria was able to marry a man she loved and live the rest of her life in comfort.

The Calleias' explanation for this sudden good turn of luck was that the money had come from a previously unknown wealthy relation who had died without any other heirs, but few people bought it. Most everyone assumed that what had really happened was that, just before he left that fateful night, Mulliner had told Gloria about the location of a treasure he had hidden nearby.

Soon the popular wisdom became that Mulliner had stashed dozens, if not hundreds, of these hidden troves around the Pine Barrens and possibly even around the whole state. If this was the case, then no one was lucky enough to find any of these hidden treasures, but that did not stop people from looking for them. Many of those who took up this search reported witnessing strange occurrences during their efforts.

Given that Mulliner spent most of his life within a few miles of the Mullica River, it isn't surprising that this was where most of the treasure hunters did their searching and where sightings of Mulliner's ghost were most often reported. Most of these reports followed the same pattern. Someone would be walking along the river, looking for signs and clues of hidden caches of loot or spots where the ground had once been dug into, when the sound of booming laughter would echo through the woods. At that point, the treasure seeker would look up and see a tall, strong-looking man standing about 40 feet away. The large man would continue laughing as he pulled out two revolvers and pointed them at the now very frightened looter. The man never spoke, but he didn't have to because the guns he held always sent the proper message and invariably convinced anyone looking for Mulliner's treasure to turn tail and run as fast as their feet would take them.

In 1850 a group of men from the town of Batso, who had spent the night drinking and discussing the legend of Mulliner's hidden fortunes, got it into their heads that the stone that marked his grave was actually where most of his ill-gotten wealth had been buried. Encouraged by the liquor they had been drinking, the men decided to find out for certain if their idea was correct or not.

It wasn't. Instead of finding a casket full of treasure, they found one full of bones. But, having worked so long digging them up, the men were loath to leave them where they found them, so they decided to take Mulliner's remains with them as a collection of grisly souvenirs, which they thought they might be able to sell.

They were less than a quarter of a mile away from the grave when their journey was interrupted by the sound of laughter. The men did not have to hear or see any more. They ran home as fast as they could and hid what they stolen away from sight. Word soon spread across the Pine Barrens that Joe Mulliner's grave had been robbed, but the men, afraid of what admitting their guilt might lead to, said nothing.

Mulliner's bones might never have been returned had the grave robbers not been haunted by the sound of laughter wherever they went. They all knew where that laughter was coming from, and they all dreaded the day they might come face to face with its creator. Finally they could take no more, and they confessed their crime to the village's blacksmith, Jesse Richards, who returned the bones to where they belonged.

Once Mulliner's remains were back in their resting place, stories of the famous spirit grew less and less frequent. Many people believe that the Robin Hood of the Pine Barrens no longer haunts the land he called home, but others still insist that they have heard the laughter that is his calling card echo throughout the forests along the Mullica River. Either way, there is one thing that the story of Joe Mulliner's life makes clear: some spirits are simply too big and too strong to ever really fade away.

The Devil's Tower

For most of their lives, Veronica, Polly, Rita and Dina had been best friends. Joined together in preschool, they had formed a bond that not even the cutest boy or most vicious slight could sever. They did everything together, much to the chagrin of their parents, who had learned long ago never to make any plans that could not accommodate the entire quartet. Had they grown up in the age of cell phones, e-mails and pagers, it is likely that their moments asleep would have been the only time they spent apart. But they were 30 years too early for that sort of thing, so they had to make do with stealing every moment they could.

Anyone who spent any time with the girls would quickly figure out two things. The first was that they were never going to allow another person into their beloved clique, and the second was that they loved starting and celebrating new traditions. Any time they did something they liked, there was a good chance they would declare it a tradition and make sure that they recreated the activity at least once a year, preferably on the same date as before. That was why on the second Saturday of every August they went for a bike ride and a picnic, and why every April 5 they would prank call Peter Anderson for four hours and then make epically messy sundaes.

And it was why they went to the Devil's Tower every October 30.

It had all started because Veronica had heard that in some places kids did really crazy stuff on the day before Halloween, which was referred to as Devil's Night. She got the idea that the four of them should do something similarly wild, but it was Polly who came up with what that would actually entail. She suggested that the four of them go over to the famous landmark outside of town, break in and tell ghost stories to each other until they were all too scared to stay.

That was four years ago, back when they were 14. Now that they were mature 18 year olds they talked about ending the tradition, which now seemed a bit more childish than they liked. In the end the pull of nostalgia proved too strong, and they found themselves sneaking into the tower one last time.

"This place never changes," said Rita as she started cleaning up the spot where they always sat. "I bet there are cobwebs in here that were here when we were 14."

"Well, it's not like this place gets a lot of visitors," said Dina. "I bet we're the only people who ever come in here."

"I wouldn't say that," said Polly, holding up an empty beer bottle she found lying on the floor, "because I know we didn't bring any beer the last time we were here."

"Yeah, I think I would remember that," said Veronica, "especially considering what happens to Rita after she drinks one."

Rita defended herself. "That happened once, and it was—like—Canadian beer, so it was super strong."

"It was still funny," Dina said as she lit the candles they always brought along with them.

Polly walked over to a corner and shone her flashlight into it. A mouse jumped at the exposure and ran away. Polly didn't make a sound. She wasn't one of those girly-girls who went all crazy when she saw a rodent or insect, unlike Veronica, who would have run screaming if she had seen the same thing.

"It's weird," Polly said as the mouse disappeared from sight, "but this is probably the last time we'll ever do this, and I think I'm going to miss this creepy old place. And you know, if this is going to be our last time here, we should honor that fact in some way."

"How would we do that?" asked Veronica.

"Well, how about, instead of telling the same old ghost stories we always tell, we tell stories about the tower?" Polly suggested.

"But I don't know any stories about the tower," said Rita, who liked telling the same old story she always told.

"Sure you do," said Dina. "Everyone in this town knows at least one story about the tower. I can think of four or five myself."

"Sounds good to me," said Veronica.

"Great," said Polly, "so that's what we'll do."

"Fine," sighed Rita, who was finished with her clean up.

Each girl sat down in her usual spot and turned off her flashlight in favor of the light from the flickering candles.

"Who's going to go first?" asked Dina.

"I will. I know a good story about the tower that my older brother told me," said Veronica.

The other three girls pulled out the snacks they had brought and poured out some cups of hot chocolate as Veronica started telling her story.

*   *   *

Terry needed a job. He had just dropped out of school, and his parents had told him that if he didn't get a job right away they were going to kick him out. None of his friends could help him get work at any of the stores, restaurants or gas stations that they worked at, so he was left to thumb through the want ads for anything that might look promising. One ad in particular got his attention: "Are you good at breaking stuff?" it asked. "If you are, then call…" and then there was a phone number.

This ad seemed to have been specifically meant for Terry, who was—it had to be said—a genius when it came to mindless destruction. He had destroyed many things in the short span of his 17 years, and the thought of turning all of that destruction into a paycheck sounded extremely appealing to him. He called the number.

"Hello, Helios Demolition," answered the man on the other end of the phone, "this is Oscar Helios speaking."

"Uh, hi, I like to break stuff," said Terry.

"I take it you've seen our classified ad, then?"

"Yeah, and I'm really good at breaking stuff."

"I'm sure you are, kid. What's your name?"

"Terry."

"Okay, Terry, tell you what I need. I'm about to start a big job this week, and some of my regular crew have gone and got themselves thrown in jail for starting a bar fight. Do you think you can start tomorrow?"

"No problem."

"Great. You'll need a hardhat and a crowbar and a way to get to the old Devil's Tower. You know where that is?"

"Sure, who doesn't?"

"Great. I'll see you then."

"Wow, this 'getting work' thing is easy," said Terry as he hung up the phone.

The next morning, Terry showed up at the Devil's Tower with his crowbar and hardhat. He was the first person there. In fact, a whole hour passed until anyone else showed up. Terry was ready to leave when a rusty old pickup truck drove up to the tower. At its wheel was a short, overweight man whose curly gray hair was in desperate need of a good styling.

"You Terry?" asked the man as he stepped out of the truck.

"Yeah," said Terry.

"I'm Oscar," the man said. "We talked on the phone yesterday."

"Yeah."

"You're a man of few words, aren't you Terry?" said Oscar.

"Huh?"

"Never mind. I'm sorry that I'm late, but it looks like we're going to be even more shorthanded than I expected. I could only get one more person to join us."

"Okay," said Terry. "And what are we going to break?"

"You're standing in front of it," said Oscar.

Terry turned around to see what his boss was talking about, but all he saw was the tower. Oscar could tell by the confusion in the boy's eyes that he wasn't making the intended connection.

"I've been hired to demolish the tower. They want to develop this land and need the tower to be cleared away."

"But how can three guys demolish a concrete tower?" asked Terry. "Are we going to use dynamite?"

Oscar smiled. "Not yet. First we're going to demolish the interior and then—when I get my regular crew back—we'll take care of the façade."

"You mean we're going inside?"

"Of course."

"But the tower—" He lowered his voice to a whisper. "I hear it's *haunted*."

"You're not very bright, are you Terry?"

"No, sir," Terry admitted honestly.

In the distance, the two of them heard the sound of a roaring engine making its way down the road.

"That'll be Jessie," said Oscar.

A minute later, Terry saw a rider on a motorcycle speeding toward the tower. He found it hard not to stare, especially when the bike stopped and he saw that its rider was a very attractive woman with long red hair.

Oscar introduced the two of them. "Terry, this is my daughter Jessie. She doesn't usually work for me, but she was willing to help me out of this fix."

Terry smiled shyly at the woman. "Hi, Jessie."

"Hey, kid," she said dismissively.

"Did you find a hard hat, sweetie?" Oscar asked his daughter.

She shrugged and lifted up her bike helmet.

"Yeah, I suppose that'll work just as good. I guess now that we're all here, we might as well get to work."

Terry was so distracted by Jessie that all of his fears about the tower being haunted had vanished from his mind. With his crowbar in his hand, he followed Oscar and his daughter inside and started doing what he was good at—breaking stuff.

As they worked, Terry started wondering about the building's history. He had heard a lot of stories about the tower, of course, but he never knew why it had been built or what it was used for before it was abandoned. While inside, they found no clues about its possible purpose.

Terry became so wrapped up in his work that he lost track of what Oscar and Jessie were doing until it was time to break for lunch. "Hey Oscar, when do we eat?" he called out, but all he heard was silence.

Terry turned around and saw that he was alone. "They must have gone upstairs," he said to himself. He walked over to the stairway and shouted up the steps. "Hey guys, when do we stop for lunch?"

His answer was the most horrible, blood-curdling scream he had ever heard outside of a horror movie.

The scream had obviously come from Jessie. Terry was torn between his instinct to be a hero and run up and rescue her and his equally strong desire to leave the tower before he could find out what exactly would make a person scream like that in the first place. Against his better judgment, he followed his first instinct. Upstairs—to his horror—he saw the body of his boss lying prone underneath a large piece of concrete.

"What happened?"

"It dropped it on him," a terrified voice whispered behind him. It was Jessie. Terry turned to see her and was shocked by what he saw. The woman he met that morning was strong and alert as anyone he had ever seen, but she now appeared to be a frail, frightened little girl. He went to her and saw that her dark red hair was now filled with long streaks of gray.

"What do you mean?"

"We were working in here when I saw this black…presence…hovering in the air. I pointed it out to Dad, and we just looked at it. Then, all of a sudden, it picked up this piece of concrete and dropped it right on top of him."

"But that's—"

"There it is!" She screamed as she pointed toward a dark, shadowy mist in front of them.

Terry grabbed Jessie and ran with her straight out of the tower. They got into her father's truck and drove to the nearest payphone and called the police and an ambulance. Sadly, the ambulance was too late to help Oscar, and the police chalked up the incident as an accident.

Other crews were called in to demolish the tower, but none of them lasted longer than a day, and eventually the developers gave up and just let it stay where it was.

Terry went back to school.

*　　*　　*

"That was a good one," said Dina after Veronica was done, "but this one is a lot scarier. I heard it from my cousin Louis."

*　　*　　*

Harry and Alice were bored. They didn't have enough money to go to a movie or get something to eat, so instead they had just driven around town looking for something to do. It was only when they happened to drive past the Devil's Tower that an idea occurred to Alice.

"Hey, park here for a second," she told Harry excitedly.

"All right!" said Harry, assuming he was about to get some action.

"Settle down," Alice deflated him. "This isn't about *that*. I just want to try something I've heard about."

"What?" asked Harry.

"They say that if you drive around the tower in reverse six times, then this ghost appears and scares you. Let's try it!"

"But why would we want to have a ghost scare us?"

"Because it's fun. Besides, there isn't any ghost—I just want to try it out. We can tell people we saw something and freak them out."

"That doesn't sound like fun to me. It sounds like something that'll be rough on my transmission."

"Oh c'mon, don't be such a spoil sport. Do this and I *might* consider the parking idea."

Harry didn't need any convincing beyond that. He started the car up and slowly began driving in reverse around the tower.

"Do you have to go so slowly?" asked Alice.

"Do you want to pay for new axles because I busted them driving fast backward on a rocky field?" Harry replied.

Alice frowned and folded her arms together as they made their way around. It took him nearly 10 minutes to do the first lap. "This is supposed to be fun," she reminded him. "It isn't supposed to take us an hour."

Harry grumbled and put a bit more pressure on the gas, increasing his speed to a less leisurely pace. The second lap took only four minutes.

"Hurry up!" she shouted.

The third and fourth laps both went faster, but were still agonizingly slow for Alice's taste. By the fifth she was rapidly growing bored of the project and was barely paying attention—focusing instead on seeing what good songs were being played on the radio. She had found something by the Stones when Harry started on the sixth and final lap.

"So how is the ghost supposed to appear in front of us?" he asked as he drove.

She shrugged. "I dunno. I think I heard someone say that she flies out of the tower screaming and takes over your vehicle."

"What? You didn't say—"

But before Harry could complete that thought, the two of them were shocked silent by the sound of a loud, horrible screaming sound. As the car edged closer to the tower's front entrance, completing the sixth lap, they were stunned to see a white figure burst out of one of the windows and race toward the car.

In his panic Harry slammed his foot on the gas but forgot to take the car out of reverse. He and Alice screamed when the ghost passed through the car's windshield as the car continued backward down the road.

Still screaming, Harry took his foot off the gas pedal and slammed on the brakes, but nothing happened. The car kept hurtling backward.

Alice screamed at him. "Do something!"

"I'm trying!" he said, but nothing he did seemed to work. The ghost appeared to be fully in charge of the vehicle.

Alice looked behind her and screamed even louder when she saw that the car was heading directly toward a very large and immovable tree. "We have to jump out!"

They tried to open the doors and leap out of the car, but the doors wouldn't budge, and their windows wouldn't open either.

"You know, Alice, this was a really stupid idea," Harry said just before the car hit the tree.

*　　*　　*

"Okay, that's my story," said Dina.

"What happened to Alice and Harry?" asked Veronica.

"According to my cousin, she was crippled and he lost an arm, although he could have said that just to make the story more dramatic. So, who's next?"

"I want to go last," said Polly.

All of their eyes turned to Rita.

"But I don't know any stories about the tower," she protested.

"Sure you do," said Dina. "Everyone does."

"Fine," Rita sighed.

*　　*　　*

Once a bunch of kids went into the tower and died because they ran into a scary ghost.

*　　*　　*

Dina frowned. "That was lame."

"I *told* you that I don't know any stories about the tower," said Rita exasperated.

"Okay," said Polly, "then I guess I'll go. I wanted to be last because I happen to know the *true* story of the tower and why it's really haunted."

"How?" asked Dina.

"My grandfather told me. He knows everything about the history of this town and all about the man who built the tower, Manuel Rionda."

*   *   *

Harriet Rionda did not want to move to New Jersey. Born and raised in New York City, she could not bear the thought of leaving her beloved metropolis for an estate in the boonies. It took all of her husband's persuasive powers to convince her that the move was in both their best interests.

"We will be free of all of this noise and pollution and be in a place with nice clean air with nothing to disturb us but the sound of our own thoughts. It is the perfect place for us to at last have a child," he said.

Harriet had long wanted a baby, but had not yet been able to conceive. Her husband was convinced that the city was to blame, and eventually she came to agree with him.

Manuel was a very wealthy man who had made his fortune in sugar. Years ago he had purchased 13 acres of land near the town of Alpine and had since added to his property bit by bit until it consisted of over 200 acres. It was time, he had decided, to start building on the property and make it his home.

Because his wife was still so hesitant about the move, baby or not, he decided to make sure her new home suited all of her needs. Knowing how much she loved the water, he built an artificial lake on the property and planted her favorite trees and flowers wherever there was room. But the true proof of his devotion came when he decided to build her the tower.

It had come to him in a dream. Because Harriet was so concerned that she would miss the sights of her beloved hometown, he would build her a monument that rose high enough above the ground that she could see some of New York from New Jersey. It would take a lot of time and money, but he was certain it was going to be worth every penny he spent.

Harriet wasn't so sure. The idea of the tower seemed like a foolish extravagance to her mind, but she knew that once Manuel was struck by such a romantic notion, there was nothing she could do to convince him to give it up.

The tower was still being built by the time the two of them moved onto the property. As the work progressed Manuel's ambitions had also grown, and he had decided to build a library on one side of the tower and a chapel on the other. It was designed to resemble something that would have looked suitable on a medieval castle, and constructing it made him feel somewhat like a king.

Despite all the fresh air and quiet, though, the two of them had no luck conceiving a child. It soon became clear that Harriet was never going to be able to bear children. This realization made her very depressed, and she started keeping to her room for long periods of time. Manuel would try to lure her out with gifts and kind words, but gradually she became harder and harder to reach.

A good man who loved his wife, Manuel had never before been the type of man to think of other women, but as Harriet grew more and more distant and left him alone for days and sometimes weeks on end, his fidelity was strongly tested. It is admirable how long he managed to keep himself from failing this test, but—given how little time Harriet now spent with him—it was inevitable that

The Devil's Tower

he would eventually fail and find himself in the arms of another woman.

Her name was Inga, and she was a maid from Sweden. She wore her short blond hair in a bob and she had the kind of shy, innocent smile that reminded Manuel of his wife. She had spent months flirting with him before he had even noticed she was there, but once he had it didn't take him long to act.

He was very discreet, not wanting to bring any shame or humiliation down upon his wife. The two of them never did anything untoward in the house. They would instead go out into the country and indulge themselves there amongst the animals and trees. They thought they were safe there and that no one would ever see them.

They were wrong.

Harriet had very seldom visited the tower that had been built especially for her, but one warm afternoon in 1922 she got the urge to see New York and decided to go up to the tower's roof for the very first time.

There she found that if she squinted her eyes as she stared through the telescope Manuel had installed on the roof for just this purpose, she could see the shape of her beloved city in the distance. It wasn't perfect, but it would do. Satisfied, she was ready to go back down when she caught sight of something in the woods below. She turned the telescope for a better look and gasped at what she saw.

It was her husband and the maid.

This sight proved too much for Harriet's fragile mental state. Denied the possibility of children, she could not bear the thought of now losing the love of her husband.

In the distance, Manuel and Inga heard a terrible cry echo from the tower.

They found Harriet's body, broken and bloody, on the ground in front of the tower. In her grief she had jumped and ended her misery once and for all.

Manuel was inconsolable. He ceased all construction on the tower and sent Inga away. He interred Harriet's body inside the mausoleum connected to the tower's chapel and did everything he could to repent for his horrible sin against his wife.

His servants soon avoided the tower, claiming that it was haunted. They reported feeling cold gusts of wind inside its walls, as well as the sound of a woman constantly crying. Manuel never came into contact with this ghost because he also refused to have anything to do with the tower after Harriet's death.

As he grew older, he started selling off his land—after the town of Alpine had amazingly rejected his offer to turn the property into a public park. Just before he died, he requested that Harriet's body be removed from the mausoleum and buried instead in Englewood's Brooklawn Cemetery. When he died he was buried beside her, but few people believe that this arrangement allowed her spirit to rest. Instead her ghost remains connected to the tower that was built for her and from which she ended her unhappy life.

*   *   *

"And that's the true story of the Devil's Tower," Polly told them triumphantly.

"I hate to say it," said Rita, "but I kinda prefer Veronica and Dina's stories to that one. At least they were sort of scary. Yours was just about a big whiner who couldn't deal with life."

"Yeah," agreed Dina. "That Harriet chick sounded totally lame. No wonder her husband cheated on her."

Veronica chided her friends. "You two are so judgmental. I liked your story Polly," she said to her friend, "although it could have been scarier."

Polly shrugged. "Sometimes the truth isn't that scary. —Are we out of s'mores?"

"I think so," answered Dina, "but I still have some twinkies."

The four girls ate their snacks and drank the rest of their hot chocolate in silence. Despite all of the ghost stories they had told inside the tower over the years, they just didn't find it a scary place to be anymore. Instead of being afraid, all they could think of was how much they were going to miss it when they were grown up and no longer able to spend all of their time together like they used to.

"We really should come here next year," Rita said.

"We'll all be at school," Dina reminded her.

"Yeah, but I bet if we made an effort, we could still all make it. It wouldn't be that hard."

"But," said Polly to Rita, "you have to make sure you have a ghost story about the tower you can tell."

"I will," Rita promised. "I will."

The Strange
Fate of Antoine
Le Blanc

Antoine Le Blanc was a man who went through many different identities: murderer, fugitive, executed criminal, medical guinea pig, collector's item and ghost. Some people believe he still haunts the home of his former employer, a building that has housed a series of different restaurants for the past 60 years. But not everyone agrees that it is his ghost that haunts the building. Some people insist that the ghost that haunts Jimmy's Restaurant at 217 South Street, Morristown, New Jersey, belongs to a young woman named Phoebe—one of Antoine's three victims. Either way, this macabre tale is easily one of the most bizarre stories ever to blossom from the Garden State.

It all started in 1833, when a man named Samuel Sayre decided he needed some help running his family farm. He was not a rich man—his grand home and fine possessions having been familial heirlooms—so he went into town hoping to find someone willing to perform such chores as cutting firewood and slopping the hogs for no wage beyond room and board.

Antoine Le Blanc was literally just off the boat when he met Sayre. A Frenchman who had come to the United States from Germany, Le Blanc spoke very little English. The 31-year-old immigrant assumed he was being offered a job as the foreman of a large farm, not realizing that the proposed position was much less prestigious. He accepted Sayre's terms even though he could not fully comprehend what they were. An educated man who had come from a wealthy family, it never occurred to Antoine that someone might offer him such menial employment.

When they arrived at the farm, Le Blanc was mortified to discover that he was expected to live in a tiny room located in the house's dark, dank basement, but it only got worse from there. He was introduced to Sayre's wife, Sarah, and their servant, a young woman named Phoebe. To Antoine's horror, he realized that he was expected to take orders not only from Sayre and his wife, but from Phoebe as well. For a man like Le Blanc, this was intolerable—not only was he not a foreman like he had thought, but he was now expected to listen to the commands of a young servant girl.

He would have quit right then and there, but the truth was that he was broke and there was nowhere else for him to go, so he swallowed his Gallic pride and went to work. He lasted all of two weeks before his ego could take no more of this tremendous indignity. As he lay in his bed one night, he thought of all the fine things he had seen stashed throughout the Sayre home; it enraged him that a man who owned such things would be so miserly as to deny him a good wage for his labors. Drunk from a bottle of wine he had stolen from the kitchen, he decided that his two weeks of work had earned him the right to take whatever he wanted from the house. And because his employer would never agree to such a deal, he would have to make sure that Sayre had nothing to say about it.

That next morning was May 11. Le Blanc woke up with a hangover and started his day the same way he had for the past two weeks. As he chopped firewood and fed the hogs, he imagined the different ways he could dispatch his employers, choosing in the end the most violent method available to him.

But first he went to the same tavern where he had met Sayre and spent the last few coins he had left to his name, knowing they would soon be replaced. He drank his fill and staggered back to the farm, arriving there at 10:30 PM. Full of liquid courage, he grabbed a shovel and called out to Sayre from the stable, insisting that there was a problem with one of the horses.

"What are you shouting about?" he heard Sayre's voice call out in the dark. He stayed quiet and waited for his employer to walk through the stable door.

"What is going on?" Sayre asked again as he entered the horses' stable.

Le Blanc answered him by swinging the shovel as hard as he could into the back of Sayre's head. The impact came so unexpectedly that Sayre didn't even have time to cry out. He fell to the ground, where Le Blanc kept hitting him with the shovel until he was certain that Sayre was dead.

Sayre's wife, Sarah, met the same horrible fate as her husband. If anything, Le Blanc made her suffer more, angry that he had been forced to take orders from a woman.

It was this same sense of entitled chauvinism that made him put down the shovel when he decided to find Phoebe, the servant girl, and pick up an ax instead. If taking orders from Sayre's wife was an incredible affront to his pride, then having to mind the word of an illiterate maid was a full-on assault. He found her asleep in her bed and made sure to wake her so that she knew the ax was coming her way.

His murderous revenge completed, he went about searching the house for everything he could carry that looked the slightest bit valuable. He started stuffing these items into a large sack he carried over his shoulder. He was so busy looting the house that he failed to notice that many of these purloined items were falling out of the sack.

The next morning, a friend of the Sayres named Lewis Halsey was on his way to visit them when he noticed some out-of-place items in the middle of the road. Upon finding a man's shaving kit that bore the initials "S.S.," Halsey immediately suspected that something had happened to his friends. He turned and rode back to Morristown to inform the sheriff. Agreeing with Halsey's suspicions, Sheriff George Ludlow organized a group of locals to ride with him to the Sayre home. There they discovered the three corpses Le Blanc had left behind.

Knowing that the Frenchman was the most likely culprit, Sheriff Ludlow rode off in search of him and found the vicious killer drinking in a Hackensack tavern. His plan had been to go to New York, where he was going to catch a boat back to Germany. His bag of stolen goods sat right by his side.

Le Blanc was caught red-handed, and he knew it. He confessed his crime in the Morristown jailhouse. On August 13 he was given a brief trial, and a jury of his peers took only 20 minutes to decide that he was guilty. Judge Gabriel Ford sentenced him to death by hanging and further added that his body would be handed over to Dr. Isaac Canfield for the purpose of scientific research.

On September 6 some 10,000 people arrived at Morristown's center square to watch Le Blanc's execution. Considering that the village at that time had a population of only 2500, it was evident that people had traveled from all across the state to witness this grisly spectacle. The crowd was so vast that many people climbed nearby trees or sat on available rooftops to get a better view of the hanging.

A special gallows had been constructed for the occasion. Instead of falling down through a trap door, Le Blanc would instead be jerked off of the gallows platform by means of a counterweight connected to the rope around his neck. The crowd cheered as the noose was slipped around his neck and roared with approval as the counterweight lifted him eight feet into the air. If the purpose of this new gallows was a quicker, more merciful kill, then it was a complete failure. Instead of breaking his neck, the process left him to dangle and asphyxiate. After a few minutes he finally died, much to the approval of the surrounding mob.

For most people the story would end there, but the world was not finished with Antoine Le Blanc. His bizarre tale did not just end because he was no longer alive.

According to the judge's orders, Le Blanc's body was shipped off to Dr. Canfield. The judge had assumed Canfield wanted the body so he could dissect it and further his studies in human anatomy, but the truth was that Canfield, inspired by Mary Shelley's famous book, *Frankenstein: The Modern Prometheus*, wanted to conduct his own experiments in using electricity to resurrect the dead. Assisted by Dr. Joseph Henry, he wired Le Blanc's corpse to a primitive battery and attempted to use the current to bring the murderer back to life. Although they succeeded in making his muscles twitch, his eyelids open

As an educated man, Antoine found it intolerable to be a mere laborer on a farm.

and his lips smile, they could not revive him, so they made a death mask of his face and—following through on a strange request from the sheriff—skinned him and sent his hide to a local tannery.

That special gallows built in Le Blanc's honor had cost money, and the sheriff needed a way to pay for it. Knowing how people would want souvenirs of the murderer's come-uppance, he devised a scheme in which Le Blanc's hide would be sent to the tannery where it would be turned into leather that would be used to make wallets, bags, lampshades and book covers. For people who couldn't afford to buy these top-shelf items, strips of Le Blanc's skin were sold on street corners. To authenticate these morbid keepsakes, Sheriff Ludlow signed all of them himself, and they quickly made their way into many Morristown homes.

For 60 years no one knew what had happened to Le Blanc's remains once Dr. Canfield had finished with them. It was rumored that the doctor had taken the body and hung its skeleton in his office, but this was eventually disproved in 1893 when a renovation on the county clerk's office revealed a hidden box full of human bones. Le Blanc's remains were finally buried, but even burial was not enough to allow his tale to come to an end.

Over a century later, the murderous Frenchman was just a hazy Morristown memory. If anybody there remembered him, it was most likely because one of the grisly souvenirs of his death had been passed down through subsequent generations, along with the tale of how the wallet or lampshade had come to be. The farmhouse where he had committed his heinous crimes was just another charming old building. In 1946 it was turned into a restaurant for the first time, and it has been used in that capacity by a number of different owners for the past six decades. And over time, each one of those owners eventually came to the same conclusion: the building was haunted.

In 1957 the house nearly burned to the ground when a kitchen accident resulted in a devastating fire. It was rebuilt with new additions that same year and soon reopened. Although there had been the occasional strange occurrence in the house before the fire, unusual happenings were now much more frequent, especially in the room that used to belong to Phoebe, the Sayres' murdered servant girl.

In the room, waitresses claimed to catch horrible glimpses of a terrified young woman screaming in the reflection of the mirror. Sometimes they were unfortunate enough to see this frightening sight when they were carrying a whole tray of food. On more than one occasion the waitresses screamed and dropped everything on the spot.

The room was also said to be much colder than any other room in the house, and waitresses claimed that they often felt a chilly pair of hands touch down upon their shoulders, which also resulted in its fair share of dropped trays and plates.

But not everything strange that happened in the house happened in Phoebe's old room. One owner was about to leave for the night when he realized he had to make a phone call in his office. He set the keys he had been carrying on his desk and made the call. When he was finished, he went to pick up his keys, only to find that they were gone. He searched around his desk to see if they had fallen off the edge, but he couldn't find them anywhere in his office. Although he was certain he had just dropped them on the desk, the fact that they weren't there seemed to prove that he had been mistaken, so he went and looked for them all around the house. After a long and increasingly frustrating hour of searching, he finally gave up and returned to the office. As he walked into the room, he heard the sound of keys dropping onto a desk and, to his amazement, found them sitting in the exact same spot he had thought he had dropped them in the first place.

Years later a different owner believed he had had a paranormal experience when—on his opening night—an expensive crystal punch bowl cracked and split apart right down the middle as he was filling it. He was the first of several owners who would hire psychics and exorcists to come in and help rid the old Sayre house of its spirits. So far, it doesn't seem as though their efforts have met with much success. Most people now agree that not only does Phoebe's ghost haunt the building, but that her murderer's spirit is a likely culprit behind some of these incidents as well.

A site of a grisly crime and a fascinating part of Morristown's history, the Sayre House will probably remain a place where odd things happen for a very long time.

The Tavern
Owner's
Daughter

Phyllis Parker, despite all of the time she spends at the Bernardsville Public Library, has yet to check out one book or take advantage of any of the other available materials. The reason for this is simple. Phyllis is dead. She has been for over 200 years, and the reason her spirit is drawn to the library has nothing to do with her interest in literature but, rather, with the building the library currently occupies. It once held a tavern, owned by her father, that was the site of an incident so heartbreaking that her spirit has yet to recover from its impact.

It was the age of the Revolutionary War, and her father's tavern was a popular meeting place for American soldiers seeking a respite from the British. There she worked as a barmaid, much to the delight of the tavern's patrons, who were all dazzled by her raven-haired beauty. Quick-witted and born with a sharp tongue, she impressed all of the men who met her with her strength and spirit. She took no abuse from any man and had thrown many a drunken lecher out onto the street, to the great amusement of the tavern's regular customers.

Even those men who preferred their women meek and retiring couldn't help but be attracted to her powerful charisma. It didn't hurt that she was easily one of the most alluring woman in the whole state. She was tall, standing nearly six feet, and the entire length of her long body was crafted with the kind of curves that can turn a grown man into an awestruck child. Her long, black hair hung down in ringlets all the way to the small of her back and her eyes were so fiercely blue that a person could see them once on the other side of a crowded room and never forget what they looked like.

Bernardsville Public Library

But with all of these blessings of nature came a price—
Phyllis could not exist without breaking men's hearts. She
did so not because she was evil or full of any kind of mal-
ice, but because she had only one heart to give, and she
had yet to find the man she believed deserved it. Not a day
went by when a man did not confess his love for her.
Some of her spurned suitors took their rejection like gentlemen, but many did not. Simply because of who she
was, Phyllis had been cursed many times; eventually, the
weight of these curses fell down upon her.

She fell in love.

With the wrong man.

*   *   *

Phyllis met Dr. Henry Byram the night he first walked into her father's tavern. It was an unusually quiet night, mostly because the powerful rain outside was keeping most of the regulars from leaving their homes. She noticed him as soon as he walked through the door, and for good reason.

The tall doctor was the first man Phyllis had ever seen who could be considered her equal. Not only because of his height—he was 6'5"—but also because of his posture and bearing. He spoke with the accent of a wealthy, well-educated Londoner, but his swarthy skin, dark hair and handsome features strongly suggested that there was some Italian in his lineage. He was the first man she had ever seen who made her feel nervous and self-conscious. He was the first man who had ever brought a blush of red to her cheeks.

"Does this tavern offer lodging?" were the first words he ever said to her.

She nodded. "My father takes care of all of that," she said in a voice that barely broke above a whisper. "I'll go get him for you."

"I would be much obliged," he said, smiling at her in a manner that made her heart race.

She found her father and brought him over to the man. They discussed the terms of his stay and agreed on the right price for the length of time the man required, which was to be several months.

"If you're going to be staying here for that long," her father said to the man, "I would like to know your name."

"Of course," the man smiled. "It was rude of me not to introduce myself earlier. I'm Dr. Henry Byram."

"It's a pleasure to know you, Doctor. I'm John Parker, but most folks call me Captain—"

"An ex-military man I take it?"

"That's right," her father said, "and I take it you've already met my daughter, Phyllis."

Dr. Byram bowed toward her. "It's an honor to meet you, Miss Parker."

Phyllis just smiled. She was too busy falling in love at that moment to think of a response.

*   *   *

For the next few days, Phyllis kept her distance from the handsome doctor. She was not used to the feelings he stirred inside of her, and she hoped that maybe if she avoided him they would go away. They didn't. If anything, they grew stronger. She started dreaming about him, both at night when she was asleep and during the middle of the day. She told no one of her infatuation and had no idea how she was supposed to act upon it. For the first time in her life she was not the object of desire, and she was not equipped to handle the problems this situation presented.

The doctor was cordial to her during their dealings, but there was nothing in his manner that suggested he thought of her as anything more than the tavern keeper's daughter. He made no attempt to flirt with her; his cheeks did not blush when they talked; his eyes never lingered on the more prominent contours of her figure—he did nothing whatsoever that indicated he might share her attraction. This potential indifference of his really did her in. Had he immediately shown any kind of affection for her, she would have probably added him to her growing mountain of rejected suitors, but by simply ignoring her, he ensured that she was his for the asking.

Dr. Byram was not a blind man. He was struck by the sensual force of Phyllis' charms the very first moment he saw her, but he knew from experience that the best way to woo a woman like her was to pretend as though he was only barely cognizant of her existence. He bided his time and waited weeks before he gave her even the slightest clue that he saw something in her to be admired.

It was another quiet evening and he was sitting at a table, eating his dinner. She approached his table with a jug of wine and asked him if he wanted her to refill his glass. At that moment he looked up from his plate and feigned a look of casual discovery.

"You really do have the most extraordinary eyes, don't you?" he asked, as if the thought had just suddenly occurred to him.

Though she never would have thought it possible, Phyllis' entire body blushed with delight. "I like them," she answered in a voice more girlish than her usual tone.

He turned back to his plate and started eating again. She turned around and floated back to the bar on a cloud of utter delight.

*   *   *

"That Byram fellow is a strange duck," Captain Parker commented as he moved one of his pawns forward on the chessboard.

"How so?" asked his friend Paul Seville, who responded by moving one of his knights.

"Well, for one thing," the captain said as he mulled over his next move, "he doesn't seem to know a lot about medicine."

"What makes you say that?"

"I've asked him a few questions about this pain I have in my leg and his answers were very vague."

"Has he ever examined it?" asked Paul.

"No," the captain admitted.

"Then how can you expect him to be more specific?"

"I suppose that's true, but I've never once seen him do anything that would suggest he was a doctor. I had a fellow collapse in the tavern a few days ago, and he just sat there and watched like everyone else. Wouldn't a real doctor get up and try to help the man?" he said as he decided to move his rook.

"Depends on his character. Just because a man has studied medicine doesn't mean he'll be more naturally inclined to help others," Paul said as he moved his queen. "Maybe he's not used to working with the living," he added.

"What? Do you think he might be one of those ghouls who spends his time looking inside stolen corpses?"

"It's possible, and those fellows tend to not be too concerned about keeping people alive—especially since they need dead folks to continue their studies."

Captain Parker thought about this for a moment.

"That would explain the long periods of time he's gone from the tavern. He could be digging up bodies and gutting them for his 'experiments,'" he said with a shudder.

This speculation made Paul laugh. "Why is it you always have to think the worst of people?" he asked his friend, who was in the midst of moving another pawn.

"Because it keeps me from being surprised whenever my suspicions turn out to be true," Captain Parker answered.

"Check," said Paul, as he took one of his friend's bishops with the move of a pawn. "You better hope that you're wrong in this case."

"Why do you say that?" asked the captain as he studied the board and realized he was only three moves away from losing the game.

"Have you not seen how your daughter looks at him?"

"Who?"

"The doctor. Who else?"

"She doesn't look at him, does she?"

"Like he was sculpted out of marble."

"I wonder what she sees in him," he said as he took Paul's encroaching pawn with his queen. "He's a handsome fellow, I suppose, but she's never been one to make decisions like that so frivolously."

"Checkmate," Paul announced with a satisfied smile.

"Blast!" swore Captain Parker. "Let's play again," he insisted, completely forgetting that they had just been talking about the doctor and his daughter.

*   *   *

"Come on, Phyllis, don't be like that," slurred the drunken sergeant who had been coming into the tavern and ogling its beautiful barmaid for the past two weeks. "Give me a kiss. I promise I won't bite."

"You've had your fill, Martin Henry," she warned him. "You best be leaving before you do something you'll regret."

Martin laughed. "I won't ever regret kissing you, I can tell you that."

"Get out," she ordered him. "I won't tell you again."

A hush fell over the tavern as everyone turned to see how the drunken soldier would respond to such a statement.

He chose rage.

"Who are you to tell me to leave?" he roared at her, but before she could answer him, he called her a name that made the regulars wince. It was a name she had been called maybe half a dozen times before, and Phyllis started to take action. Her response was always the same. It hurt like hell—watching it, that is. Having it happen to you probably felt a whole lot worse.

But before she could raise her leg back to set the kick into its proper motion, everyone heard the sound of a chair toppling over and watched as the drunken sergeant was lifted off of his feet by Dr. Byram.

"What did you just call this fine woman?" the doctor hissed at the smaller man.

The sergeant lied. "I can't recall. I wasn't thinking. Words just came out of my mouth before I knew what I was saying!" he insisted tearfully.

"You impugned her honor and suggested she was a woman of easy virtue," the doctor said to remind him. "If I were you, I would take it back and apologize immediately before something happens to you that would require the amputation of an extremity."

"I'm sorry, Phyllis," the sergeant apologized. "I didn't mean to call you a—"

The doctor glared at him. "Were you actually going to say it again?"

"No!" the sergeant answered. "I'm sorry! Really I am! I take it back. I really do!"

Dr. Bryam dropped the smaller man to the ground and turned and saw a look of utter amazement on Phyllis' face. She had grown so used to defending herself that she had forgotten how thrilling it could be to watch someone else do it for her. He smiled at her and then looked down at the weeping drunkard at his feet. "Now do as she told you and get out! And neither of us ever want to see you in here ever again."

The sergeant nodded tearfully, staggered to his feet and ran out of the tavern as fast as his unsteady legs could manage.

"That was—" Phyllis struggled for words. "That was wonderful."

"It was my pleasure," he said with a smile.

*   *   *

From that moment on, the two of them were a couple. Within a month, they were engaged. Captain Parker said nothing about their relationship at first, but when his daughter told him that they were going to be married he remembered the conversation he had had with his friend Paul.

"But how much do you know about this fellow?" he asked, after she noticed the hesitancy apparent in his face.

"I know he is a good man who loves me," she answered. "Isn't that enough?"

"Not by a long shot," he said, shaking his head. "For all that you know he could be a murderer or a bigamist or an English spy. The only thing I'm certain of is that he can't really be a doctor, if his habits are anything to go by."

"That's nonsense!" said Phyllis. "How could you even think such things?"

"Because I'm old enough to know the ways of this world," he replied. "They can be very cruel, especially in matters like this. It is the heart of foolishness to marry someone before you know who he truly is."

"But I do know! You're the one with all these doubts."

"It is a father's obligation to have such doubts. I hope they are wrong, but what kind of parent would I be if I didn't ask you to learn more about the man you plan to give yourself to?"

Phyllis' anger faded away, and she gave her father a long hug. "I love him," she said.

"I know you do, but sometimes that isn't enough."

*   *   *

As the war continued, many important men sought a night's refuge in Parker's tavern, but no one more so than General Anthony White. A tall, imposing man whose charisma made him a natural leader who had earned the fierce loyalty of his troops, General White was the man the leaders of the American forces counted on to execute their most important and dangerous missions. He expected nothing less than flawless precision from himself and his men, and it was for that reason that he had been assigned to transport and protect a series of important strategic documents. The loss of any one of them could mean the eventual defeat of the American rebellion—to lose them all would make that defeat a virtual certainty.

These vital documents were all kept in the pouch that was strapped over the general's shoulder as Captain Parker led him into his room.

"Tell me," asked the general as he looked around, "do you have anyone else staying here who I might be wise to keep my eye on?"

Captain Parker hesitated for a moment as he considered the question and whether it was right to answer it the way his instincts suggested.

"There is a man," he said finally.

"Who?"

"My daughter's future husband."

The general raised his eyebrow. "You have cause to find him worthy of suspicion?"

"Nothing concrete," Parker said, "but I advise you to keep an eye on him just the same."

"What is his name?"

"Dr. Henry Byram. He's a tall fellow, like yourself. He speaks with a very posh accent, but looks more like a Roman than a Englishman."

"Byram, you say?"

"That's right."

"Thank you, Captain," said the general. "I hope for your daughter's sake that your suspicions are without merit."

"So do I, General White. So do I."

*   *   *

As meticulous as General White was, his perfect success rate when it came to missions had as much to do with his willingness to take risks as it did with his attention to every detail. There was something about Captain Parker's description of Dr. Byram that seemed uncomfortably familiar. That was why, when he went back downstairs to eat with his men, he deliberately did something he normally would never do—he left the documents he had been ordered to protect with his life in his room, available to anyone who wanted them. It was an enormous gamble, but the potential payoff was more than worth it.

When he returned to his room, the documents were gone. Without missing a beat he turned around and found Captain Parker, who led him and two soldiers to Dr. Byram's room. He knocked on it softly and waited for it to open.

The look on Dr. Byram's face when he saw who was standing at his doorway was one of both surprise and resignation. "Hello, Anthony," he said softly.

"Aaron," the general replied to his greeting.

"Aaron?" asked Captain Parker.

"Yes, I am sorry to say with some certainty that this man is not a doctor named Byram. His name is Aaron Wilde, and his activities as of late have meant the deaths of many American soldiers."

The imposter shrugged. "I do what I can."

The two soldiers pushed past him and started searching his room for the stolen documents. They found them in a space in the floor, underneath a loose floorboard.

Enraged, Captain Parker slapped the spy across his face. "How could you be so deceitful? What have you done to my daughter's heart?"

Wilde stayed silent. He had nothing to say.

*   *   *

"I'm going to enjoy this," Sergeant Martin Henry said as he slipped a noose around the traitor's neck.

"Not as much as I enjoyed seeing you weep like a child at my feet," Wilde whispered. The sergeant slapped him for his insolence, but the spy did not react.

"Do you have anything you want to say?" asked General White. He hated this part of his duties, but he knew that—for the greater good—he had to carry it out.

Wilde thought for a moment. He then turned to Captain Parker and spoke his last words. "Tell her that I'm sorry. I lied about who I was, but not about how I felt."

Sergeant Henry looked over to General White, who gave him a nod. The sergeant kicked out the chair that Wilde was standing on. The rope jerked taut, and the spy was dead.

"What shall you do with him?" Captain Parker asked the general.

"Leave him to rot," answered White. "His body will send a message to all those who would consider imitating his treachery." The general turned away and headed back to the tavern so he could get some sleep.

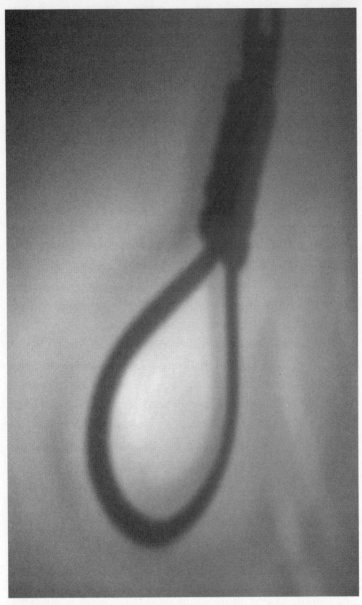

"I'm going to enjoy this," Sergeant Martin Henry said as he slipped a noose around the traitor's neck.

Captain Parker stayed where he was and stared at Wilde's hanging body. All he could think about was how his daughter was going to react when she saw the man she loved left hanging in the town square for carrion to feast upon. The thought was too much for him to bear. He could not let the general's order be fulfilled.

He found Paul and a few others. Together they cut down the body and placed it inside a makeshift casket. They had no place to bury it, and, because the captain was too tired to think about the matter any longer, they lifted up the casket and started carrying it back to the tavern.

*   *   *

Phyllis was cleaning up when the door opened and her father came in, followed by a group of men carrying a long wooden box.

"What's going on?" she asked as they placed the box on the closest table.

"Nothing for you to concern yourself with," he answered.

"Is that what I think it is?"

"Yes."

"Who's in it?"

Captain Parker paused. He could not bring himself to tell her. "A traitor," he said. "Now leave it at that and go to bed. It has been a very long day."

*   *   *

Phyllis did as she was told and went to bed. She was tired and fell asleep almost immediately, and her mind turned to dreams. She dreamt that she was asleep in her bed, where the sound of a man's cries threatened to wrest her from her slumber. She dreamt that the screams grew louder and louder until she could stand them no longer and finally opened her eyes. She was in her bed and listened to the screams and realized that she knew where they were coming from: Henry.

In the dream, she jumped out of her bed and ran toward her beloved's cries. "Save me, Phyllis! Save me!" he said. But no matter how fast she ran she could not save him, because he was not there. "Where are you?" she cried out in her dream. "I can't find you! Where are you?"

Her dream ended when she heard his answer. His words rocketed her awake.

"I'm in the box," he told her. "I'm in the box."

*   *   *

Phyllis ran downstairs to the tavern. She tried to open the box with her bare hands, but it was nailed shut. She went outside and found an ax, then used it to smash the box to pieces. When she saw what it contained she began to scream. Those screams awoke the entire neighborhood.

Her father was the first one to find her—her face a red mass of tears, her eyes lost in a haze of impossible sorrow.

"What have you done?" she said. "What have you done to him?"

Her father stayed silent.

"What have you done?" she screamed one last time. Then her nerves finally gave out, and she collapsed to the floor.

*   *   *

Phyllis never recovered. Decades passed, and she only sank deeper into the madness that first overcame her that night. Her insanity took its toll on her beauty, and when she finally died there was no sign whatsoever of the incredible charisma that had once made her one of the most desirable women in the world. No one mourned her passing.

*   *   *

A century later, the tavern was no more and the building was now a private home owned by a young couple named Frank and Emily Morgan. Frank was a salesman whose job required him to leave Emily alone for long periods of time. She didn't mind his absences when they first got married, but they became harder for her to deal with following the birth of their first child, a girl they named Mary.

"Something has happened to this house," Emily told her husband the one day, just after he came back from a week-long trip.

"What now?" he asked, assuming the roof had sprung another leak or one of the windows had been broken.

"I don't know," she admitted, "but it just isn't the same as it was when we first moved here."

"I don't understand."

"At night," she explained, "the atmosphere is much more ominous than it ever used to be. I don't like it."

"I didn't know the house even had an atmosphere," said Frank.

"That's because you're always asleep by eight o'clock," she told him. "Try being here when Mary wants to be fed at three in the morning, and you'll find out that this place is far spookier than it has any right to be."

"I'm sure it's just your imagination," he said dismissively.

"Even if it is," she answered back, "I'd prefer to live somewhere that didn't give my imagination so much to work with."

*   *   *

Two weeks later, Emily found herself alone once again inside the gloomy old house, and—because of the storm raging outside—the tension she felt was even worse than usual.

She had just put Mary to bed, which normally would mean trying to catch some sleep for herself, but she was in that strange state she sometimes fell into where she felt too tired even to sleep. She pulled out some sewing she hadn't been able to get to since Mary was born and sat down on the couch in the living room to work on it. Within 10 minutes of sitting down she was asleep, and the house was silent save for the sound of her ladylike snores.

KER-THUMPPP!

The loud sound roused her from her sleep. She recognized it as the noise the heavy front door made when someone opened it too quickly. It was followed by the sound of footsteps—a lot of them, far more than one man could make.

"Frank?" she shouted out into the darkness.

There was no response.

Her apprehension grew as the footsteps moved closer. She tried to get up and hide, but she was too scared to move. Her terror turned to confusion when the footsteps were obviously only a few feet away, but she saw no one in front of her.

WHAAAAMMMM!

Emily jumped as the sound of a large object dropping onto a table echoed throughout the room. Her heart raced as she tried to figure out what to do next. Her answer came when she then heard the sound of an ax chopping into wood. She stood up and ran into Mary's nursery and locked the door behind her. At that moment she heard the sound of an agonizing scream, which woke up the baby, who immediately started crying. Emily ran to pick up Mary and tried to calm her down even though her own nerves were rattled. The screaming continued for far longer than Emily thought she could bear until, at last, it stopped, and the house was silent once again.

Refusing to stay in the house a second longer, Emily grabbed a suitcase and packed it as quickly as she could. She then carried it and Mary a full two miles to the closest hotel, where she stayed until Frank returned from his latest trip. When he returned to an empty house, Frank was surprised to find pinned to the front door a note from his wife explaining where she was. He immediately went over to the hotel to retrieve her and was shocked by her adamant refusal to return to their house.

"I'm not going back there. Not now—not ever."

"What is wrong with you, Emily?" he asked disbelievingly. "Have you lost all of your senses?"

"Don't insult me!" she shouted. "You weren't there! You didn't hear what I heard that night. If you had you wouldn't be trying to convince me to go back there— you'd be selling that horrible place to the first person willing to buy it!"

"Okay," he relented. "Tell me what happened. Help me to understand, because right now I just don't get it."

"It started with the door opening, and then I heard footsteps—a lot of them, like they were coming from a group of men. I thought they were burglars, but I saw no one! Then I heard the sound of something being dropped on a table and the sound of an ax chopping through wood. That's when I ran to the baby and that's when I heard it…"

She stopped, as if she could not bear to recall that horrible sound. Tears began to stream down her face as she relived it once again.

"What did you hear?" Frank asked her gently, confused by this emotional reaction.

"It was a wail of pure anguish," she answered. "It was a scream of terror and madness. It echoes through me still. I feel it in my bones—it aches. I could feel its hopelessness and despair. Do you know what it was, Frank? That sound I heard? It was the sound of the end of the world—the end of everything. I will not go back to that house. I will not hear it again."

*   *   *

It took him a month, but Frank was finally able to convince his wife to return to their home. In order to do so, he had to find a new job—one that would not require him to travel. It was his promise that he would be with her each night that finally convinced her to break her vow to never enter that old house ever again.

A year passed without incident. Frank believed that the nonsense was behind them and their lives were back to normal, but all it took was one conversation to change his mind. It happened when he invited a business acquaintance named Charles Webb over to the house for supper. Webb had seemed unusually intrigued when Frank had given them their address, but it wouldn't be until after they had eaten that he would find out why.

"This really is the place," said Charles as the two of them sat in Frank's study to share some brandy and cigars.

"I'm glad you like it," replied Frank, assuming Charles was simply complimenting the house.

"No," Charles said. "You misunderstand me. What I mean is that this place really is the same building I suspected it was when you gave me your address. This really is the old Parker Tavern. Did you not know that?"

"No," answered Frank. "Is that something significant?"

"Depends on what you think is significant," said Charles. "In terms of history, the tavern was an important meeting place for the local American forces during the Revolutionary War, but I'm more interested in the part it played in the story of Phyllis Parker and her traitorous lover."

"Who?"

Charles looked genuinely surprised. "Do you mean you've lived here all this time and don't know what happened here?"

"I suppose so," Frank answered with a shrug. "So what happened?"

Charles then told him the story of what happened when the tavern owner's beautiful daughter fell in love with the handsome doctor. Frank listened politely throughout the first part of the story, but he truly became interested in what Charles had to say when he got to the part where Wilde's body was returned to the tavern and discovered by his lover. Suddenly Emily's story made sense, and—for the very first time—Frank knew that it was not simply the result of her overactive imagination. She had really heard all of those noises she had described, and he had refused to believe her.

Overcome with guilt and shame, he got up from his chair and left Charles alone in the study. He found his wife, who was putting Mary to sleep, and he hugged her as tightly as he could.

"What's come over you?" she asked as she hugged him back.

"I'm so sorry," he whispered. "I should have believed you."

"About what?"

"This house. This horrible house," he answered. "We can't stay here. I know that now."

Frank put the house up for sale the very next day.

*   *   *

Eventually, the building was turned into a public library, and, though there was never another incident like that experienced by Emily Morgan that frightening night, it was no secret to the people who worked there that the library was haunted by one of its former residents.

The evidence of this paranormal presence usually came in the form of invisible footsteps or the sound of a dress swishing past the bookshelves when nobody was around. Doors and windows opened on their own accord, and different staff members had experiences as unique as Emily's.

Librarian Maria Mandala was alone in the library late one night finishing up some necessary cataloguing when she heard the sound of a woman humming an unrecognizable tune behind her. She turned and saw that no one was there. The tune persisted, but now it came from another part of the library. Maria followed it to the Mystery section, but found only empty space. She returned to where she had been working, and when she heard it again she left it alone, having deduced that it was most likely coming from the library's famous phantom.

Although Maria was nonplussed by this particular encounter with Phyllis, another experience did send a chill down her spine. Once again she was working alone in the library late at night, when she looked down at the phone on the desk in front of her. Although she had not heard it ring, she saw that one of its lights was flashing, indicating there was someone waiting on that line. She picked up the receiver and pressed the flashing button.

"Hello?" There was no answer. "Hello?" she asked again. "Is anyone there?" No answer.

Annoyed, the librarian was about to hang up when she noticed that another button was flashing. She pressed it.

"Hello?" Silence. "Hello?"

Again, she looked down and saw that yet another button was now flashing. She pressed it and once again got no response. She looked down again and saw that now all five of the phones lines were flashing, with people waiting to talk to her on all of them.

This sight so unnerved Maria that she dropped the phone and ran out of the library. She spent the next few minutes trying to calm herself down, and when she finally succeeded she went back inside to the sound of the disconnected phone beeping over and over again. None of the lights were still flashing, so she hung up the phone and tried going back to work, but she was too spooked to continue. A few days later she contacted the phone company to see if anyone had actually attempted to call the library that night. She wasn't at all surprised when they told her that no one had.

Martha Hamill, another librarian, had an equally spooky experience while working after hours in the library, but hers was harder to explain, given the site's haunted history. Like Maria, she had been at work doing some cataloguing, when she heard children whispering around her, sounding as though they were busy trading secrets. She left her desk and found that she heard the sound throughout the building, until, out of the blue, it just stopped; she didn't hear it again. Of all the paranormal events experienced at the library, this one was perhaps the strangest because there was nothing in the building's

213 The Tavern Owner's Daughter

history to explain the presence of so many secretive child spirits.

Despite having had such an obvious presence in the building, the ghost of Phyllis Parker has only made herself visibly apparent on two occasions. The first of these two encounters occurred when a young rookie policeman named Joe Maddaluna was walking by the library late at night. Though he was still new to his beat, he had walked past the library enough times to recognize when someone was working there late and when it was empty. That night he saw a beautiful young woman standing in front of one of the library's windows. He had never seen her before, and—given that all of the library's lights were off—he suspected she was an intruder.

He went to the building's front door and found that it was open, so he let himself in and made his way over to the window where he had seen the beautiful woman standing. She wasn't there when he got there, so he started searching among the library's shelves to see if he could find her. A few minutes passed, and he was about to give up when he noticed her standing in the same spot he had seen her before.

"Please stay where you are, Miss," he spoke to her. "I want to ask you some questions."

The woman turned to look at him, but before he could reach her, she vanished out of sight, disappearing as if she was never there.

The young policeman got out of the library as quickly as he could, but he was so curious about the incident that he went back during its operating hours and asked if the building had a history of being haunted. He then found out the story of Phyllis and Dr. Byram and discovered that he may well have been the first person to see the ghost since her death two centuries earlier.

Only one other person has seen her since. It happened a few years later when a young boy, who had been taken to the library by his mother, came running to her and started excitedly talking about the "pretty lady" who had done the "really neat trick." His mother forced him to calm down and tell her what had happened, and he told her how he had seen a beautiful woman standing in front of a window—the same one where Officer Maddaluna had spotted the spirit before—looking sad.

"I said hello to her," the boy told his mother, "but she didn't say anything back. She just did the trick."

"And what was that?" asked his mother.

"She went *poof*," he answered, throwing his hands up into the air.

"She exploded?"

"Nah-uh, she went *poof* and she was gone!"

"She disappeared."

He nodded excitedly. "Yeah, she diseappeared."

The boy's mother then went to the library's front desk and told them what her son said he had seen, and they told her about Phyllis and also about Officer Maddaluna.

"Did you hear that, honey?" she asked her son when they had heard the whole story. "You saw an actual ghost."

"Neat," said the boy. "Can I have some gum?"

The Little Devils
Part III:
The Devils Revealed

Donny was visibly disgusted by what he had just heard. "Are you telling us that the Jersey Devil grew inside of a dead woman?" he asked Max.

"According to this, he did," Max affirmed, nodding as he held up the book from which he had been reading.

"But that's horrible! What kind of legend is that? It's so totally gross!"

"It's not gross," said Max, defending his story. "It's cool. According to this legend, the Jersey Devil is the product of pure hatred and rage, caused by two soul mates being forever torn apart by society!"

"What?" asked Donny, wondering where Max had found the intelligence to make such a statement.

"Well, that's what it said in the story's introduction," Max admitted. "I didn't read you guys that part because it was pretty boring."

"The story I read is a lot better," Donny said.

Max couldn't believe his ears. "Are you kidding? It was so lame! Mine had sex in it!"

"So did mine!"

"Where?"

"Mr. and Mrs. Shrouds had to have done something for them to have that 13th baby."

"But that was before the story even started! In my legend, it happens in the middle, when you can think about it."

"Look, there's only one way we can settle this."

They both turned toward Andy, who had long ago tuned them out and had started leafing through the latest issue of *The Fantastic Four*.

"What?" he asked when he noticed they were both staring at him.

"Whose story was better, his or mine?" asked Donny.

"They were both good," Andy said noncommittally.

"Come on," sighed Donny. "One of them had to be better than the other."

"Why can't you two ever agree on anything?" asked Andy. "I'm tired of always having to settle things."

"This'll be the last time, we promise," said Max. "Which one was better?"

Andy frowned and put his comic book down. He then reached over and grabbed the book he had been reading from earlier.

"What are you doing?" asked Donny.

"I'm going to tell you guys what I learned about the Jersey Devil," Andy told them.

"But you haven't given us an answer yet," said Max.

Andy ignored him. "The stuff I read didn't say anything about where the Devil came from, but it told me a lot about the different times it has been seen around the state. It also has some theories about some more practical explanations for these encounters."

"So you're not going to tell us which story you preferred?" asked Donny.

Andy ignored him and started reading from the book. "When discussing the history of the Jersey Devil, one must break it down into three separate periods. The first would include all sightings of the Devil that came before 1909, most of which are anecdotal at best and poorly documented. The second, and shortest, period would consist solely of all of the sightings that occurred during

1909, the year in which reports of the Devil were at their highest. In fact, the Devil was sighted more times that year than in all of the other years of its known existence combined. And finally, the third and final period is made up of all of the sightings that were reported in the years that followed the second period. Although the sightings in this third period are all as well documented as those in the second, they occur with much less frequency—at a rate of about once or twice a year."

"That can't be true," Max said. "My brother Frankie said he saw the Devil four times last year alone."

"Yeah," answered Donny, "but you're forgetting the fact that Frankie is a big fat liar."

Max was about to defend his brother, if only out of familial instinct, but after he thought about it for a second, he had to concede the point—Frankie *was* a big fat liar.

"Can I continue?" asked Andy.

"Sure," said Donny, "though I have to say your book is a lot more boring than the ones we read from."

Andy ignored him and continued. "The best known of the first-period sightings is said to have happened some-time in the early 19th century. No specific date is avail-able, but the story involves an important figure in New Jersey naval history, Commodore Stephen Decatur. Needing new cannon for the ships in his fleet, the com-modore had decided to test the latest models on a local firing range. He and his men had spent half of the morn-ing firing cannonballs into the sky when he noticed a strange creature flying in the air in front of them. At first he assumed it was a kind of misshapen crane, but once he got a better look at the creature, he could tell that it bore no resemblance to any kind of bird he had ever heard about. His men soon saw it as well, and, before he could tell them to stop, they had aimed a cannon in the creature's direction and fired upon it. Everyone watched as the cannonball sailed into the air and, by some small miracle, actually met its target. As astonishing as this feat of aim was, everyone was much more shocked to see that the cannonball appeared to have had no effect on the flying animal, as it continued on its way—no worse for wear."

"So the Devil is invulnerable, just like Superman," said Donny. "We better take a note of that. I mean, if a cannonball can't slow him down, what is one of our lousy BB guns going to do?"

"Good point," said Max, who grabbed a pen and started writing in the notebook he always kept in front of him during these meetings. "Devil is invulnerable, must find out its weakness," he quietly whispered the words he was writing down.

"The second best-known first-period Devil account is famous less for what happened than it is for who it happened to. Sometime between the years of 1816 and 1839, it is believed that Joseph Bonaparte, the former king of Spain and brother of the French emperor Napoleon Bonaparte, visited the town of Bordentown, New Jersey, to go on a hunting expedition. When he returned from this trip, Bonaparte claimed that he had been confronted by a strange creature that he had first confused for a deformed bird, but, when seen up close, proved to be something else entirely. He claimed that he had been able to take a shot at the creature, but his bullet appeared to have no effect on the monstrous animal."

"What do they mean 'sometime between the years of 1816 and 1839'?" asked Donny.

"I guess that's the closest they can narrow it down to," Andy answered. "I guess the people who lived in Borden-town back then weren't very good record keepers."

"They were pineys," said Max. "It would have been a miracle if there was anyone in that place who could read or write."

"Don't say that about pineys," said Donny, whose parents' families had, unlike Max's and Andy's, both come from the Pine Barrens. "It's prejudiced."

Max apologized, if only because he knew if he didn't Donny would respond by saying something anti-Semitic, and he would be forced to punch him, and they wouldn't talk to each other for two weeks. This had happened before.

Andy started reading again. "During the years of 1840 and 1841 the Devil was blamed for the deaths of an unusually large number of livestock across the state. Because there was no sign of an increase in the popula-tions of the usual predators, people looked to a new explanation for the rise in these incidents. Reports of these animals being found dead immediately following the sound of a horrible—almost human—scream, as well the presence of unidentifiable tracks at the scene of these crimes, led people to speculate that it had to be the work of the Jersey Devil. Nearly two decades later, people claimed to have seen the Devil whisk away livestock in towns across the state, including Haddonfield, Bridgeton, Smithville and Leeds Point. People became so afraid of the Devil in the Pine Barrens region that they frequently refused to leave their homes after sunset."

"You mean they wouldn't even go outside once it became dark out?" asked Max incredulously.

"That's what it says," Andy said. "But according to the book, this didn't last, because after the Devil was spotted hanging around the New Jersey–New York border by a guy named George Saarosy in 1894, it wasn't seen again for another 15 years."

"Where did it go?" asked Donny.

"No one knows," answered Andy, "but by 1903 people started to believe that it was gone forever. One guy named Skinner, who wrote about legends and myths and stuff, told everyone that the age of the Devil was over and no one would ever see or hear about it in New Jersey ever again."

"Wrong!" yelled Donny.

"Yeah, he definitely was, because not only did the Devil come back, he came back *big time*!" To prove his point, Andy started reading directly from the book once again. "After a decade and a half in which not a single report of the Devil was recorded, the monster returned with a vengeance in the third week of January 1909. During those exciting seven days, over 1000 different people— from southern New Jersey all the way to Philadelphia— reported seeing the winged creature."

"A thousand?" asked Donny and Max at the same time.

"That's right," said Andy, who then continued reading from the book. "January 16, 1909, was a cold and gloomy Saturday, much like any other winter day when the sun was reluctant to shine. Thack Cozzens, a resident of the town of Woodbury, was leaving his house that morning to visit some friends when he looked up and saw a strange creature flying in the air. At first, like so many others, he thought it might have been a deformed bird of some sort, but then he saw that the animal's eyes glowed red in a manner that was not of the natural world. Although he was just a small child when the Jersey Devil had last been spotted around Woodbury, Thack knew the creature when he saw it. 'Devil!' he cried out. 'It's the Devil! He's back!' Apparently caught off guard by his shouts, the creature quickly flew away, just as his neighbors started emerging from their homes to see what all the fuss had been about."

"I bet they all thought he was crazy," said Max.

"Stop interrupting me," Andy admonished before he started reading again. "At first many of his neighbors thought he was delusional, but as the days passed it became clear to all of them that Thack had not imagined what he had seen that morning. The next day, in the town of Bristol, the Devil was spotted by a man named John McOwen, a patrolman named Sackville and the town's postmaster, E.W. Minister. Sackville was so caught off-guard by the monster that he barely had time to pull out his sidearm and fire a few shots at it before it flew away, screeching its horrible cry. As the day continued, many residents of Bristol noted the sight of strange hoof prints in the snow around them. Two expert animal trackers were brought in to investigate, and both admitted that they had never seen tracks that resembled those found there that day. By Monday these same tracks were found in towns throughout the area. Not only were they found on the ground in Burlington, Columbus, Hedding, Rancocas and Kinhora, but people also reported finding the monstrous hoof prints on the tops of their roofs and on the branches of trees. In Burlington a posse was formed to follow the tracks, but the group's efforts failed when their hound dogs refused to follow the trail."

"Dogs are smart," said Donny. Max agreed.

Andy ignored them and continued. "Despite all of this activity from the Devil, it wouldn't be until the 19th that someone got a truly good look at the monster. It was 2:30 in the morning, and Nelson Evans and his wife were sleeping soundly in their bed when they were suddenly awoken by the sound of wings flapping against their bedroom window. Rising from his side of the bed, Nelson hurriedly lit the lamp he kept on his bedside table and looked outside the window to see what was causing all of the noise. The next day he gave the following account to the local authorities: 'It was about three and a half feet high, with a head like a collie dog and a face like a horse. It had a long neck, wings about two feet long, and its back legs were like those of a crane, and it had horse's hooves. It walked on its back legs and held up two short front legs with paws on them, I tell you, but I managed to open the window and say, "Shoo," and it turned around, barked at me and flew away.'"

"He said 'shoo'?" asked Donny incredulously. "The Devil can't be hurt by cannon fire, but you say 'shoo' to it and it flies away? I don't buy it."

"That's what he said happened," said Andy.

Donny shook his head. "He was lying. I bet he saw the Devil and screamed like a girl and hid under his bed until his wife told him it was safe to come out."

"That makes more sense to me," agreed Max.

"Listen you two," Andy said, starting to lose his patience. "I was quiet when you guys read your stories. I didn't interrupt you all of the time."

"Sorry," both of his friends mumbled.

"Now I've lost my place!" Andy said with uncharacter-istic impatience as he looked down at the book he was holding. Usually he dealt with his friends' natural ebul-lience with the grace of a saint, but today they were twanging away at the very last of his nerves.

"You were at the part where wussy-boy is lying about how he scared away the Devil," Donny reminded him.

"Thanks," Andy said through gritted teeth. He found the spot where he had left off. He started reading again. "That same afternoon two professional hunters from Gloucester were hired to track the beast. They followed the creature's tracks for 20 miles before they finally gave up. That evening, a group of people in the town of Camden saw the Devil perched on a tree branch. They reported that when it realized they could see it, the monster barked at them and then took off into the air. The Devil's reign of terror continued on to the next day, when it was spotted once again in Burlington by a young police officer, and then in Pemberton where the Reverend John Pursell reported to a local paper that he had 'Never seen anything like it before.' Posses were formed in Haddonfield to search for the monster, but they were stymied when the tracks they were following ended abruptly, leaving no further clues as to where the Devil had gone. Another posse, this one organized with folks from Collingswood, did little more than watch as the creature flew over their heads on its way to neighboring Moorestown. But before the Devil reached Moorestown it made a stop at the Mount Carmel Cemetery in Maple Shade, where it was seen by a man named John Smith. Smith's report of seeing the creature

Illustration of the Jersey Devil, based on the description by Nelson Evans in 1909.

was backed up by a man named George Snyder, who insisted he had seen a creature with the exact same description just a few minutes later. The Devil also made a stop at the town of Riverside, where its hoof prints were found on roof tops and circling around the body of a murdered puppy."

"This thing murders puppies?" asked Donny, a look of horror etched on his face.

Andy shrugged. "That's what it says."

"There isn't anything more evil than killing a puppy," Max declared.

"Except for killing a lot of puppies," Donny said.

"Well, duh," Max said, "that goes without saying."

Donny ignored him and turned to Andy. "Why would the Devil kill a puppy?" he asked.

"Maybe it was hungry," answered Andy.

"Hungry? You mean this thing eats puppies?" asked Max, who seemed shocked by the very idea of it.

"You've got to remember," Andy explained to his friends, "the Jersey Devil is an animal, so it doesn't understand that you're not supposed to eat puppies."

This explanation made sense to Max and Donny, so they let Andy go on.

"On Thursday the 21st, a whole street trolley full of people saw the Devil fly over them in the town of Clemington, and all of their descriptions matched those made by others since the Devil's reign of terror had begun that previous Sunday. As news of this spread to other towns, trolley drivers in Trenton and New Brunswick were instructed to carry weapons, though none of them ended up having to use them. In West Collingswood the local fire department tried to fire their water hose at the Devil, but missed the creature. Some of them regretted their actions when it appeared that the Devil was about to turn around and charge directly at them in retaliation, but, much to their relief, the monster seemed to think better of it and turned around and flew away. But the most ominous of the Devil-related happenings that day occurred along the Delaware Valley. All throughout the week chickens had been going missing, but that Thursday all of the farmers were shocked to discover all of their birds dead on the ground. What made this even more shocking was the fact that not a single one of them bore any kind of physical injury. They had simply died on the spot without any explanation."

"I bet they were frightened to death," said Max.

"Ah, that's stupid," argued Donny. "How can a chicken be frightened when it doesn't have a brain?"

"Chickens have brains," Max answered back.

"Yeah, but only little teeny-tiny little ones that aren't big enough to handle things like emotions."

"Okay then, how do you think they died?" asked Max.

"The Devil killed them with an evil look. It's the only way that makes any sense."

Before this argument could go any further Andy cleared his throat, and they both got his message. He went on. "In Camden that night, a widow named Sorbinski heard the sound of her beloved German shepherd fighting with an animal in her backyard. Acting on instinct, she grabbed a nearby broom and ran outside to beat away the creature attacking her pet. It was only when the animal released her dog from its grip that she realized she was face to face with the Devil. Her screaming awoke the neighborhood, and everyone rushed out with shotguns and other weapons as they heeded her cry of 'Devil! Devil!' Over 100 people surrounded her house and listened as a monstrous cry led their attention to nearby Kaigan Hill. They all ran toward the hill and fired at the creature, and though some of the shots hit it, it flew away before it could be killed. After that everyone went back home and stayed inside for several days afterward. By then the people of New Jersey, particularly those that lived in the Pine Barrens, were now so afraid of the Devil that schools and factories were closed simply because almost no one was willing to leave their homes to go to work. Luckily for the business owners of the region, this paranoia proved to be short-lived. After this nearly weeklong rampage throughout the state, the Devil was only spotted one more time later that year.

"Since then the Jersey Devil has been seen much less frequently, though the creature's presence can still be felt. For example, in 1927 a cab driver named Klassen was on his way to pick up a fare in Salem when his car blew a tire. While he was replacing the tire, a giant creature, which looked like a deformed bird with the head of a dog, landed on the hood of his car and proceeded to shake it violently. Terrified for his life, Klassen abandoned his car and ran until he found help. When he returned with a group of people, they found that the creature was gone, but that its distinctive prints had become dented into his car's hood."

At this point Andy paused, expecting one of his friends to interrupt him as they usually did.

"Why'd you stop?" asked Donny after a couple of seconds. "Keep going."

"Yeah," agreed Max. "It's finally getting interesting."

Andy went back to reading. "In the winter of 1951 the people of the town of Gibbsboro reported that for two days they were under siege from the creature, though it ended up not doing anyone any harm. Remarkably, considering the amount of fear the Devil has caused over the years, there has yet to be a single reliable report of a person being killed by the Devil, though there have been some close calls. One good example of this occurred in the spring of 1961 when a group of teenagers had the experience of a lifetime as they sat parked in a car in a quiet section of forest commonly reserved by the local youth for amorous activities. The two couples were engaging in some innocent foreplay—"

Andy couldn't stop himself from sniggering with his friends before continuing. "—when they were rudely cut short by the sound of a loud, horrible screech coming from above their heads. To their amazement they watched as the soft top of the convertible was suddenly shredded into pieces. Looking up, they could now see through the torn roof a strange dog-bird hybrid hovering above them. With a loud bark it dipped its long neck down the hole in the roof, but before it could get its head inside the car, all four of the teenagers had jumped out and started running for safety. They stayed away for an hour before returning to the car to see if it was now safe. The Devil was gone, but it had done some serious damage to the car's interior before it had left. Five years later, the Devil was considered the most likely suspect when a Delaware Valley farm suffered the loss of 31 ducks, 3 geese, 4 cats and 2 dogs in one day."

Andy cleared his throat before he started reading the final paragraph of the chapter. "Given all of this evidence of the Jersey Devil's existence, one is compelled to ask two obvious questions: what is it and where did it come from? Unfortunately, neither of these questions has yet to be answered in any satisfactory way. Some people insist that the creature that looks like a deformed bird is actually just that—a deformed bird. Others talk about the legends that theorize that the Devil is a deformed human warped by the sins of its parents, while many simply believe that it is the embodiment of pure evil. In the end all of this is purely speculation, and all we know for sure is that this is a mystery that will remained unsolved for a very long time."

Andy put the book down, and Max took over with his pen and notepad at hand.

"So," Max said as he looked at the notes he had jotted down since they had started, "this is what we know about the Jersey Devil. It lives in New Jersey. It has wings and kind of looks like a mix between a whooping crane and a collie. It might have been the son of a woman who wished that her 13th child 'be a devil,' or it might be the son of a woman who died cursing the people of this area. Its appearances are unpredictable and sporadic—" Max took a moment to smile, delighted by his use of such big words "—except for one week in 1909 when everyone seemed to see him. Let's see, what else?"

Donny reminded him. "It eats puppies."

"And might be the embodiment of pure evil," added Andy.

"Puppies, evil," Max said as he wrote those points down. "Hey, what time is it?" he asked, suddenly aware of how long the three of them had been at this research.

Donny looked at his watch. "Yikes! It's 5:37!"

Both he and Max jumped out of their chairs, knowing they were late for dinner and seriously risking the ire of their mothers. "Meeting adjourned until tomorrow!" Max announced before he grabbed his stuff and ran out of the clubhouse. Donny quickly followed him, but Andy lingered behind. His family didn't eat until later in the day, and besides, he had something else to attend to.

He decided to leave the heavy books behind and grabbed only his satchel, which was filled with some apples and carrots. He closed up the clubhouse and ambled slowly to his own special, super-secret spot—one that not even Donny and Max knew about. It had required some construction on his part, and he collected the materials from all of the same spots that the friends had mined to make the clubhouse, but it was much smaller and much more private. He had built it several months ago when, entirely by accident, he had made an exciting discovery.

It had happened at night while he was supposed to be asleep but was instead leafing through a copy of one his older brother's *Playboy* magazines under his covers with a flashlight. While reading about Vicki Peters (aka Miss April), he heard a noise outside.

It was the sound of a gunshot, which was unusual, especially at this time of the year. Curious, he put down his flashlight and magazine and got up to look from his bedroom window. He couldn't see where the shot had come from, but considering the length of its echo, it could have been made quite a long way away. He was about to go back to bed when he heard the sound of something thudding roughly to the ground outside his window.

From what he could see, it appeared to be a wounded bird. It had probably been what someone had been shooting at. He decided it was in his best interest to investigate.

As quietly as he could he snuck out of his house, not daring to wake his parents. He made it out no problem, but almost foiled his own efforts; he almost screamed when he saw what lay in front of him on the ground.

All of the descriptions were correct. It did look like the unholy union of a large crane and a dog. He knew enough about his monsters to recognize it instantly. It was the Jersey Devil, but with one difference—it didn't look evil or monstrous. It looked like what it was: a wounded animal. So he decided to take care of it.

"Hiya boy," he greeted it as he entered his super-secret hiding spot. "I got your dinner. I heard you like puppies today, but all I got is the usual apples and carrots."

The Devil barked happily at the sight of him and eagerly started gnawing on the food being offered to it.

Andy had considered telling Donny and Max about his find, but then they had decided to start that monster-hunting club of theirs, and it occurred to him that they might not be ready just yet. In the meantime he thought it would be best to keep them distracted with books while he himself learned more about his strange new friend.

"So tell me, boy," Andy asked as the Devil chewed on an apple, "was your mother really dead by the time you were born?"

The End